Shuffletown USA
A Multi-Voice Memoir

by
Judy Rozzelle

2004

Parkway Publishers, Inc.
Boone, North Carolina

available from:
Parkway Publishers, Inc.
P. O. Box 3678
Boone, NC 28607
www.parkwaypublishers.com
Tel/Fax: 828-265-3993

Library of Congress Cataloging-in-Publication Data:

Rozzelle, Judy.
Shuffletown, USA : a multi-voice memoir / by Judy Rozzelle.
p. cm.
ISBN 1-887905-85-5
1. Charlotte Region (N.C.)—Social life and customs—Anecdotes.
2. Charlotte Region (N.C.)—Biography—Anecdotes. 3. Charlotte
Region (N.C.)—Social conditions—Anecdotes. 4. City and town
life—North Carolina—Charlotte Region—Anecdotes. 5. Community
life—North Carolina—Charlotte Region—Anecdotes. I. Title.

F264.C4R697 2004
975.6'76—dc22
2003027868

Cover Illustration by Gail E. Haley
Cover Layout and Production by Aaron Burleson
Editing, Layout and Book Design by Julie Shissler

Contents

Faulkner.
Memories Are Heirlooms
Grandfather Rozzelle
There Was Usually A Reason For An Odd Sounding Name
Card Games
Shuffle To Shuffletown
Official State Sign
An English Peddler
Odd Names
Snuffytown
Shuffletown Sprang Up Around A Crossroads
The Guardian Oak
The Catawba River
Shuffletown Families
Ancestors
Sturdy People
Eli Wallen
It Was A Property Dispute
Bad Memory
Jack Cameron Returns
The Grant Sisters
Jim Crow
Work Began At A Young Age
Basket Babies
The Gabled House By The Crossroads
Dogtrot House
Did You Ever Eat Cooter?
Cousin Kissey Lived In The Big House
Cousin Kissey Bakes A Cake
Cousin Kissey's Ford Coupe
The Night I Was Born

Home Remedies
J.E.R.K.
Growing Up Country
Cousins

Cameron Circle
This Is How It All Started
Quick Trot Brownies
Turkey Trot
It Was Christmas Eve
Reindeer On The Roof
Prancer And Dancer
I'd Rather Eat Crow
Sweet Revenge
A Prank To End All Pranks
Surely, Our Wives Were Joking
Tragedy Strikes And The Brick Is Buried
Uncles
Cameron Christmas Tradition

Helpmates
Bud And Libby Clockman
The Clockmans' Passing
Rev. Sloan Baptizes His Wife
The Bain Family
Mary Bain's Miscarriage
Murder On The Dead-end Road
The News Spread Like Fire
The Funeral
Mary Bain Goes To The Hospital
Jenny Grant, 75, Marries
Old Maids?
The Wallace Women
Marriage Did Not Agree With Yvonne
Judy Liked Wearing Wedding Dresses
Vernon And Smiley Rozzelle
Elizabeth Mcmillan Rozzelle

Mt. Island Shopping Center
William Alexander (Pop-pop) Rozzelle, Jr.
Irs Audits Good Used Cars
Catfish Jumps
Shuffletown Posse
Baloney Burgers
Evening Tide

Sunday Was Once A Day Of Rest
Sunday Morning At Cousin Kissey's
Brush Arbor
A Chapel Is Built
Pearl Harbor
Gail Played The Marimba
Harry Lifts Weights
Harry Cleans His Gun
Sunday Pranks
The Carnivore Keeshonds
Communion Wafers

Mutt Sets Off The Alarm
A Brand New Fire Truck
The Fire Siren
The Screaming Siren
Town Limits
In 1966, I Had A Green Mustang
The Fire Chief
The Fire Chief Faints
The Animal Breather
Burning Mamie And Esther Gaines' House
Vfd Assists Jenny And Gg Grant
The Buddy System
Cotton Sets Himself On Fire
Cotton's Secret Barbeque Sauce Recipe
Burning Duke's

What Happened Is This

I came upon a time in my life when everything was chaos and failure. I did not have any place to go or turn to, but home. Home was Shuffletown, a pocket community that sprang up around a crossroads.

I had run from this crossroads community most of my life. But this return trip would be different. I arrived home in the middle of the night at the age of fifty and fell asleep in the bedroom I had slept in as a child and a teenager. It was in the fall of 1989 and by the spring of 1996, I had a complete change of heart about this small, uniquely American community named Shuffletown. I have written this book as an ode to all small American communities, for they are all vanishing. To live in these small places taught us all we ever needed to know about life and living.

Shuffletown is my home and this is her story. The characters' names have been changed and their characteristics have been jumbled. I have kept the Rozzelle family name as it appears on the bridge, the road and the North Carolina map. But I have changed everything else. If you are from Shuffletown or anywhere else, I hope you have fun trying to figure out which story is completely true, or which character is a real person. This could turn into quite a treasure hunt. Enjoy.

This is a memoir told in many voices. I wrote each page of the book after I went from home to home gathering the stories. The only exceptions are Gail Einhart Haley's memories of Shuffletown. She also grew up in Shuffletown and I was delighted that she wanted to add her memories to mine.

Gathering the stories for the book was a wonderful adventure. I got to really know my old neighbors and friends during these visits as we shared stories and memories. This book gives each an opportunity to speak of life in Shuffletown from their point of view.

The only thing that is totally true in this book is that I grew up in an oddly wonderful place, in a special time, raised by hardy, resilient folks and neighbors who had known my family for generations. People just are not that lucky anymore.

Judy Rozzelle

A Disclaimer

All recollections in this book occurred in the past or present or could shortly occur and happened exactly as told or bear only a faint resemblance to the truth and are as valid as promises flung towards the heavens in moments of dire fear and panic or fleeting gratitude. Characters and names in this book resemble no one living or dead, the unborn, or the unknown. Every written word came out of the author's strange and unmanageable brain.

Dedication

These stories are for all who shared the land hereabout called Shuffletown. They are dedicated to the first one awake each morning, the last one asleep, the first-born, the last-born, and all the children in between. They are for those who didn't have a lick of sense, those who never kept a promise, the lazy and no-good, the uppity, the pillars of the church, and the members of the choir. They are for the many who prayed for you and those who prayed with you, and all who prayed for rain and for the rain to cease.

The stories are for those who worried for their children and buried their children. The ones that came to visit, the drunkards, the broken-hearted, the unfortunate, and the gossips. God bless this village of odd and regular folks, saints and bigots. They are all to be honored...and remembered. They abided in the years of yesterday and taught us to shoulder today.

Dedicated especially to Lee Ryan, Melinda M. Marshall, Jodi and Casey Coffin, and the Rozzelle family.

Miami

Georgia

South Carolina

Charlotte

Myrtle Beach

New York

Dead End Road

Long Creek

Pond

Rozzelle's Ferry Road

GREATER SHUFFLETO

Long Creek

Ohio

Huntersville

ILLUSTRATION BY GAIL E. HALEY

1. William (Pop-Pop) Rozzelle Family Home
2. The Gaines Sisters' Century Old Gabled Home
3. Tad Rozzelle Family Home
4. Shuffletown Grocery, est. 1946
5. Mack Gillis's Store
6. Duke's Repair Store
7. Cotton's Paint and Body Shop
8. Shuffletown Grill, Home of the World Famous Baloney Burger
9. Harrison Rozzelle Family Home
10. Sloan Volunteer Fire Department
11. Abe Franklin Gillis Family Home
12. Rowan Hall
13. Sloan Memorial Church
14. Church Cemetery, Resting Place of Shuffletown Ancestors
15. Dogwood Plantation
16. Rozzelle Ferry Inn, The Big House
17. Rozzelle Ferry Bridge
18. Wilson Family Home
19. Ed Rozzelle Family Home
20. Cameron Circle
21. Fuller Family Home
22. Shuffletown Dragstrip
23. Eli Wallen Family Home
24. Dead-end Road
25. Jenny and GG Grant's Home
26. Abandoned Church
27. Dr. Robert Griffin Family Home
28. Francis Aaron Family Home

Home Again, Home Again

When I returned to Shuffletown for the last time, thrice divorced and flat broke, Aunt Anne balanced my checkbook, babysat my dog, Gracious, and Aunt Mutt invited me to Sunday dinner. She sat me in my Cousin Yvonne's seat. Yvonne had recently died of ovarian cancer, at the age of 49. Yvonne was Aunt Mutt and Uncle Harrison's only daughter, and my beloved first cousin. The loss of Yvonne was still unreal and we all largely ignored the depth of this tragedy.

Gathered around us for the weekly Sunday dinner were Teeny, Yvonne's only daughter, Teeny's husband, Cotton, and their children. We would make small talk over mashed potatoes and pass the pitcher of sweet tea. Finally, when the dishes were cleared and there was nothing left of the spice cake but crumbs, we would tell Yvonne stories, and I was the keynote speaker. Dinner was finished only after a proper accounting of a tall tale from the days of Yvonne's life that gave laughter to the children and tears to the adults. They captured the essence and spirit of the grandmother who died when they were too young to remember her. These stories also told them about life and living, about self-reliance, how to create humor in tense situations and the importance of determination and ridiculousness. When we share stories, it is like pulling a warm comforter around our shoulders on a cold winter morning.

One Sunday Teeny turned to me and asked, "Please, write the stories down for me and my kids. I do not want to forget them, because if I forget them Mother will fade away to just another name on a limb in a family tree. Then she will be forgotten."

I began to write down the tall tales and quiet moments between two cousins who had alternated between loving and hating each other. During this process, Yvonne sprang back to life and whispered in my ear. This was the genesis of this memoir.

As I recorded the tragic-comic history of Cousin, it became clear that it was not just Yvonne who needed to be saved from oblivion but also Shuffletown. In the years since her death, the Shuffletown we had known our whole lives was vanishing. Shuffletown was disappearing into the abyss of urban sprawl sometimes known as progress.

Shuffletown was not a perfect place. I once considered it an outpost of civilization. Still, it was home and in many ways, Shuffletown defines my life. This growing place, this community of folks, aunts and uncles, cousins and friends, neighbors, saints and bigots, is vanishing as surely as fog before the morning sun. Markers that herald change are appearing in spaces formerly occupied by home and crops. The fields, blanketed in summer with weeds, wildflowers and butterflies, are now parking lots. What began slowly with rumors of realtors in the neighborhood is now stark reality. Twenty-four hour convenience stores, grab-and-go restaurants and branch offices are taking over Shuffletown like an epidemic.

I was not living in Shuffletown in 1968 when they burned down the century-old house that belonged to Mamie and Esther Gaines and built in its place a 24-hour convenience store. I moved back briefly to Shuffletown in 1970, but I was gone, again, by 1972.

I had returned when Abe Franklin Gillis's place was sold to a major grocery store chain in 1986, but another future husband distracted me.

But I sure as hell did notice when construction soon began on a four-lane highway running from Charlotte to the Catawba River.

Ninety-nine acres of the old Spurrier farmland was sold shortly and Northwoods, the first large housing development, was started on Mount Holly-Huntersville Road in 1989. They invited the women of the church to decorate their show houses (model homes) for Christmas. In what seemed like only a moment, the Wallace family sold hundreds of acres of land on Pump Station Road, and an upscale development was built on the Catawba River and named "Overlook" by an advertising executive.

Some began to notice the changes and neighbors formed the Mt. Island Neighbors Association to protect…Shuffletown? While I thought it was a great idea to circle the wagons before the onslaught of progress and I admired their success in detouring a gravel pit from being built not far from the crossroads, I was bothered that they did not call it the Shuffletown Neighbors Association. I knew that Uncle Tad Rozzelle would have taken offense to this slight. I suspected it had to do with the seriousness of it all, but I was still offended.

Rozzelles responded to progress by forming a posse of relatives and riding into town to appear before the City of Charlotte commission. We wished to halt progress, but as Aunt Ann always said, "The only constant is change." We knew we could not stop growth. Our request to the commission was to have the old Rozzelle Ferry Inn House, built in 1849 by our ancestors, declared a historic preservation landmark in order to save it from the bulldozers.

They replied affirmatively so quickly, they must have thought we were packing heat. Even the developer who bought the land where Rozzelles Ferry Inn stood seemed all right with the idea. He jumped at the chance to purchase the land when Cousin Kissey's last will and testament was less than sensible. With that accomplished, I got married for the third time and left Shuffletown. That was 1987.

I was home again by 1990 involved in the heartbreak of divorce. The first year of the century's final decade, 1990, was a very bad year: Cousin Yvonne died in February and was buried on a dark icy afternoon; in September Hurricane Hugo ravaged the county; in November some wicked unknown person burned the Rozzelles Ferry Inn down to the ground.

We were together again that December to bury my father, William Alexander Rozzelle. Within five years, we would lose Uncle Tad and Aunt Mabe Rozzelle and five more cousins who died too young.

November 1, 2000, almost a complete decade after Yvonne's death, her brother Michael Harrison Rozzelle, joined her in death. I sat with Aunt Mutt and Uncle Harrison as they buried the last of their children. A year later, Uncle Harrison died of a broken heart. That fall I lost another cousin, Barry Hart, and another cousin, Sally Jo Thompson, lost her husband and almost her life in an auto accident. The world was out of sync. It was a dark decade for the Rozzelle family and the disappearance of Shuffletown had begun.

The Charlotte city limits ran out from the city and swallowed Shuffletown crossroads like a red tide. I was notified by mail that the name of the road in front of the house, my father's house, would no longer be named Rozzelle Ferry Road. The official name on all state and civic maps would now be Belhaven Boulevard.

I did not know a family named Belhaven, nor did anyone else. Some copywriter who was paid by the city had without feeling or research erased my family's contributions to the area. Then I heard rumors that the name of the Rozzelles Ferry Bridge was to be changed. I was fighting mad. But then an unexpected thing happened to me. Cancer.

Cancer brought the world into laser-sharp focus. Shuffletonians came to call bringing comfort and casseroles. A group of friends I had tagged as "the grumpy old women of Shuffletown" invited me to join them at inexpensive restaurants. While Martha Gillis figured out how much each one of us owed for dinner (including tax and tip) on her rhinestone calculator, we became friends. I found my strength and determination from the kids who once rode with me on hayrides to sing carols, from elders who taught me Bible verses and remembered my parents.

Tender, caring nurses who belonged to Sloan Memorial Presbyterian Church checked on me and changed my bandages. Shuffletonians nurtured me and I defeated cancer.

I began to listen to their voices and hear their stories anew. I saw the kindness in their faces and discovered that they were also often awakened at 2 a.m. by the feral hounds of hell whispering thoughts of doubt and fear into their ears.

Memories are our most precious heirlooms. They give us strength. It is in the calling of their names, not just the dates they walked on this earth, that keeps their spirit alive. The voices of our ancestors are stilled in silent graveyards, but our voices are alive ... for now. As a bulwark against inevitable change, I have written this memoir of Shuffletown, and it is told in the voices of cousins, neighbors, ancestors and friends.

Generations yet unborn must know from hearing the stories that there was a place called Shuffletown, and of those who called it home. This collection of stories is the only gift I have, to say thank you. God bless the kinfolks and neighbors of Shuffletown, who always met me at the door, fed me supper, and let me browse through their refrigerator.

Judy Rozzelle

Origins

Think of all that has happened here, on this earth. All the blood hot and strong for living, pleasuring, that has soaked back into it.

William Faulkner, Big Woods

Grandfather Rozzelle

In 1840, my great, great grandfather bought the ferry and a few years later built a house nearby. William A. Rozzelle and his wife Elizabeth not only founded the clan that bears their name, but gave the name to the road that still runs from the crossroads to the bridge across the Catawba. The first bridge over the river was built around 1850 by the State. In 1861 began the War of Northern Aggression, and near the end of the war, the Yankees burned our bridge down. The ferry business thrived.

Will Rozzelle Jr.

There Was Usually A Reason For An Odd Sounding Name

Shuffletown is a strange name, but once there were many places with odd sounding names. Just up the road there once were places called Frog Level, Three Pistols, Peach Hollow, Emmy Town, and Pig Squeal. These names were given to places for good reason. In the spring, the peach trees in Peach Hollow exploded in blossoms and it was a good place to take a date. Emmy Town was where Uncle Emmy's family settled, don't know who Uncle Emmy was, but that's how it got its name. Frog Level had something to do with bullfrogs and the river. You won't find these places on maps anymore and that's a shame.

Now you take a place called Shuffletown, supposedly in 1859, Rezis W. Spurrier bought 60 acres from R.S. McGee and that included three corners of the crossroads. Back then it was only a place where two wagon trails met. Spurrier and Sam Oglesby built a store in the northeast corner where Bud's Plants now stand. They built a blacksmith shop, a sawmill and a cotton gin and they called the place Spurrier. There was a post office in the store and mail was brought out by horseback on Tuesday and Thursday.

Sam knew a Mr. McDonald up around Huntersville who had a contract with the U.S. Government to supply four barrels of liquor to the Navy Yard in Charlotte. The contract allowed McDonald to sell any liquor left over. Oglesby purchased a keg every week and sold a dipperful for a nickel to the farmers on Saturday. This was when the farmers came to the store for mail and supplies.

Seems the wives didn't like Sam's refreshment. It is said that the women used to say that after they got a dipper full of Uncle Sam's liquor the best their husbands could do was shuffle home. So each Saturday the farmers began to say they were going to shuffle. Somebody even made up a rhyme about it.

Where did you get your liquor?
Where did you get your dram?
I got it at Shuffle
I got it from Uncle Sam.

I like this story; no matter how it happened, the name Shuffletown stuck to this place like glue, but there are other versions.

William Alexander Rozzelle, Jr.

Card Games

Shuffletown is named after all the card games people used to play around here. It was the place where World War I soldiers came to play setback, rook and, I guess, poker. It had nothing to do with liquor.

Ethel Smith

Shuffle To Shuffletown

I heard it was called Shuffletown because of all the slaves that shuffled to the Sam's store to pick up supplies for their owners. After the war, some of them settled with their families and their mules where all the colored families live now. Down there, where the old Rozzelle Ferry Road bends off the new highway and curves by Sally Davis's house.

Henrietta Grant Somers

Official State Sign

When I heard tell that they were trying to change the name to a regular name like Cook's Community, I thought that was dumb. After all, the church and the fire department are already named after the Preacher. I got in my car and drove to Raleigh, talked to a few state senators I know real well, and first thing, you know we had the name Shuffletown on the state map. I went back to Raleigh in a week and picked up an official state made sign that said Shuffletown. I planted that sign in my front yard right at the crossroads and it is still there today.

Tad Rozzelle, Proprietor Shuffletown Grocery, Est. 1946

An English Peddler

My father, Abe Franklin Gillis, told me an entirely different version of how this place got its name and I believe his version is correct. He had five sisters so he spent right much time hanging out at the old Spurrier store at the crossroads.

The store was where men gathered and gossiped. Baxter Johnson was one of the men that also visited the store on a regular basis. According to Dad, there was an on-going checkers game at the store. Far as I know, they did not even play cards.

But according to my dad, one day an English peddler stopped by the store. He had a buggy full of stuff he wanted to sell to Mr. Spurrier. He tied his horses out front, came inside, and said, "What might this place be called?" That is exactly what my father said he asked. The peddler had a heavy English accent.

"Spurrier," someone bent over the checkerboard answered. "This is old man Spurrier's place."

The peddler looked around the store and the premises. At that time in the back of the Spurrier's store, there was a place set up for an ironmonger. The ironmonger made most everything that needed steel back there from horseshoes to plows. The peddler came back in and said, "You ought to call this place, Sheffield, after Sheffield, England, where they make iron." Dad said they just thought he said, Shuffield, and the name was mispronounced and guessed at until it became Shuffletown. It was a name suggestion made by an English peddler just passing through. I don't know if he sold anything that day but he left his mark.

Abe Gillis

Odd Names

In the 50s, when Sloan's Volunteer Fire Department was organized, a few people tried to change the name of Shuffletown to Sloan. They wanted to name the place after the town's first circuit preacher, Reverend

Winston Sloan. I told them that when an odd name sticks to a region, you should keep it and be proud of it. No one signed the petition.

Rev. Kenneth Pattershall

Snuffytown

It never fails. If I'm somewhere in Charlotte and someone asks me what part of town I'm from, I don't dodge the question. I step right up to the plate and say "Shuffletown." If I saw one of those folks at a later time, they always introduced me as "Judy, the girl from…." They would pause long enough for me to hear their brains bending, then brighten and say "Snuffytown," or something worse. Usually I tried to remind them I was from Shuffletown. I told some people that it was named after a very sacred mountain in Tibet. Some people believed me.

A boyfriend once sent me a postcard from Florida addressed to my rural route number and, instead of Charlotte, he wrote Shuffletown, NC. I still have that card somewhere. I have never stopped claiming this crossroads village as my home. It made me feel special in an odd sort of way.

There aren't any real boundaries to Shuffletown, no signs saying "you are entering Shuffletown," or "you are leaving Shuffletown." I couldn't ever pinpoint what made somebody a Shuffletonian except their state of mind. Then, one night several years ago, after I had moved down the road to my new house, I was surprised to hear the Monday night eight o'clock siren from the Volunteer Fire Department. It made me feel so good that I decided along with state of mind the one qualifying rule of thumb was that if you could hear the fire siren, you were a Shuffletonian. You know, like the citizens of London were Cockneys if they could hear the bells of St. Mary's when they rang.

Judy Rozzelle

Shuffletown Sprang Up Around A Crossroads

Historically crossroads were magical places that attracted musicians, storytellers, traveling road shows, gypsy caravans, snake oil salesmen and peddlers of every ware and eccentrics of every stripe. But the folks that settled here were good people. We were plain hardworking Americans. Maybe we were a little set in our ways, but who isn't?

The road running east and west connects two towns already on the map Mt. Holly and Huntersville and so it is named after them. The road running north and south, Rozzelles Ferry Road, was named for the ferry, which my ancestors operated across the Catawba River. Rozzelles Ferry Road leads into Charlotte and since anyone around here can remember that has always been the name of the road. The name stuck to the road and the bridge after the ferry was replaced in the 1900s.

Truthfully, I believe if you traced the roads far back into history, you would find that the roads were Indian trading paths. We always turned up arrowheads and rock when we plowed our fields. The bridge was known as Rozzelles Ferry Bridge, but every thing is being renamed now in deference to new development. Even the river is now referred to as Mt. Island Lake instead of the Catawba River. I suppose the name change allows them to charge more for real estate property.

Everything that once was around here is being wiped out by new development. I am not against progress, but I do hate to see all these centuries-old roots vanish. We weren't the most prestigious part of town, but I just don't see how getting rid of Shuffletown will make the world a better place. But I don't know everything. You just have to trust God and live life day by day.

Frank Rozzelle

The Guardian Oak

The largest oak tree in the world stood sentinel in the right corner where the two roads intersected and it cast a soft shade on all who passed. Seemed like at mid-day that tree shaded most of the county. When I was a kid, some of us climbed up in that tree and dropped water-filled balloons onto passing cars. There weren't too many cars back then and we were high up in that old tree.

Harry Rozzelle

The Catawba River

The Catawba River was always a passageway. The Catawba Indians believed the river provided the spirit with a passageway to the next journey. In the 1700s, ironsmiths from west of the river loaded their goods on barges that took them down to Charleston, where they were shipped to the world. Originally, the crossroads were Indian trading paths that led to and from the river. In 1816, the Abernethy family established a ferry across the river. The ferry was a flat-bottomed barge with low sides, and they would pull it across the river with ropes. The price for a ride was a nickel for a man on a horse, and a person on foot was a penny. For the longest time the ferry was the only way to get across the river.

Bob Griffin

Shuffletown Families

This crossroads community was settled by a handful of families: Rozzelles, Camerons, Spencers, Abernethys, Gillises, and Wallens. One look at a family's Bible around here and it is apparent our forefathers didn't believe in courting a woman further away than their horses could ride in an evening. I think that explains our resilient character.

The Coopers, a black family, moved here in the early 1900s, owned 120 acres of land across from us. I played with the Cooper boys every day of my childhood. In the summertime, we swam buck naked in Long Creek. We even jumped off the bridge when a car wasn't coming. When our chores were done, we explored the woods. We found a couple of stills and climbed up in trees to watch where bootleggers stashed their hooch. I am not telling whether or not we tasted it. The Coopers were bricklayers and farmers. Their daddy lived to be 110 years old.

Most of the other black folks lived on Dead End Road off Mt. Holly Huntersville Road just past the crossroads toward Mt. Holly. Francis Aaron lived at the end of the road with his 13 kids. Francis, our local blacksmith, was half-Indian and half-colored. On Sundays, he preached at a black church up the road a piece.

The Grants lived down there also. Old Elijah Grant was the man to see when hog-killing time rolled around. He knew more about preserving meat than any other person in these parts. He was practically a hog whisperer. He'd talk to the hogs to keep them calm before we shot them. He had a skill that smart farmers respected in these parts. He could make the best cuts, and he knew how to preserve the meat. Elijah worked hard and saved his money, that's how he bought land around here. Elijah even had an A-Model Ford and the only one in the family that could drive it was his girl, Jenny. She'd drive all around the place and she was so short you had to look real hard to see her behind the wheel. Nobody cared as long as she didn't hit anything.

His girls worked just like men. They plowed and picked cotton all day. Their mother used to walk more than five miles one way to clean a woman's house. I guess she had to walk so far because no one around Shuffletown could afford to pay her. I'd see her walking over Long Creek Bridge early morning and coming back across it late at night."

Coloreds and whites were respectful of each other in Shuffletown. We all farmed out in Shuffletown. Living off the land and the whims of the weather is a great equalizer. If it didn't rain during the growing seasons, black families got just as hungry as the white families.

Times were hard in the south for a long time, Negroes and white folks on farms had to work together. When times were good we shared, but mostly times were hard. Folks were poor in these parts for more than a hundred years after the Civil War; so poor it took us a long time to notice the Depression.

Anyhow, kids never pay much attention to differences unless they are told to notice. I guess that's why when I built the drag strip I let the coloreds race right beside everyone else. Other drag strips made the coloreds race at the end of the day. Hell, sometimes they had the best cars and I wanted a good show for the folks who bought tickets.

Hank Wallen

Ancestors

Our ancestors were three brothers who were struggling highlanders lured from Scotland to Ireland in the 1600s. They left Ireland to come to America because they were angry with King James I for his restrictions on their flax and linen trade. They came down the wagon trail from Pennsylvania and settled around here. Later, they joined Hopewell Church, but they were asked to leave because they imbibed. So, you could say that, early on, Camerons didn't go to church a lot.

Jarrell Cameron

Sturdy People

All of us are descended from a long line of people who wanted to live. Times were so hard that I guess that bred a little strangeness in our blood…like the English and Frank Dellinger.

Eli Wallen

Eli Wallen

Eli Wallen, he was something else. When I was growing up, he was the trash man. He picked up the garbage we couldn't burn and dumped it in the old gold mine shaft in his front yard. But if you saw him on a weekend, he would always be dressed up like a dandy in a white suit.

When I was a teenager working at the service station, I guess he had retired, 'cause every afternoon at two o'clock you could hear Eli's tractor coming down the road. You could set your clock by it. I'd hear the tractor pull in; I'd pop open a can of malt liquor and set it on the counter. Eli would come in, drink two beers and if anyone else was standing there he would bet them a dollar he could bite the head off a twenty penny nail. You ever seen a twenty-penny nail? It's a big sucker. And he could do it and he did it fast. He'd collect his dollar, get on his tractor and go on back down the road.

Rob Griffin

It Was A Property Dispute

Did anyone ever tell you Eli Wallen bit his neighbor's finger off during a property dispute? Yeah, it was the person the Fullers bought their place from. Had something to do with where Eli strung his barbed wire fence. Anyhow, the family asked that they be kept out of this, but I knew him and he and Eli were always arguing. After the last argument, he had one finger that was only a stub. Everybody knows about it round here in the older generation, just don't tell no one who it was for the family's sake. They're good people and I wouldn't want to embarrass them.

Abe Gillis

Bad Memory

I don't rightly recall whether I ever bit off a man's finger or not.

Eli Wallen

Jack Cameron Returns

Jack Cameron is not young when he returns from the war. He is weathered in the way that country people are from exposure to wind, weather, and fatigue. He has been at war, and though wounded in body and spirit, he has survived. He does not know what he is returning to, if indeed he is returning to anything, he has known before. Jack's Celtic ancestors experienced the Battle of Culloden, the Revolutionary War and now he has seen death during the Civil War.

He was a prisoner of war in New York State and walked home. He stopped at the end of the driveway and called to his wife that he was home, to bring a change of clothes. His clothes were so covered with lice and other varmints; he burned them in a fire where he stood, before he could touch her. Jack Cameron is everyman and soldier. You find him in every culture.

Gail E. Haley

The Grant Sisters

The Grant sisters, Jenny and G-G, lived on the Dead End Road in what was once the old colored school house. Henrietta Grant Somers, their sister, lived next door in her little white clapboard house. They had something to do with raising most folks in these parts, which explains why most of us turned out in a way that made our parents proud. Well, there was Tommie Somers and me.

Tommie Somers was a big boned woman with an easy laugh who cared little for propriety. Mom and Dad hired Tommie to help with me. I was a child born with eczema. For the first three years of my life, I screamed and itched night and day. They kept me alive with a brown tar based salve, a lot of love and patience, and when they had to, they tied my arms loosely to the crib so I couldn't scratch.

Momma often said, "Tommie put salve on you and taught you to sing when you were itching the worst. Some nights she refused to go home and swung you on the front porch all night.

She would put you on her shoulder and climb the sycamore tree in the back yard to stop you from crying. If I could not find you and Tommie, I knew where to look. I would go in the back yard by the pasture fence where the big tree stood and look up through the limbs. The two of you would be half way up the tree sitting on a limb. You would look down at me and laugh. You loved it.

When you were sick and cried, so loud they could hear you in the next county. Tommie cried just as loudly. When you screamed in pain and frustration Tommie screamed also. Her hollering and her screw-up faces would eventually get you to stop crying and laugh. People knew about you two nuts throughout the county. Neither one of you were normal."

But when Tommie's husband died, she needed more money to merely exist and she had to go to work for Cousin Kissey at the Big House. Momma hired Henrietta Grant Somers, Tommie's sister-in-law, to take care of her girls. I was six and new sister, Anne, had just been born.

I knew something was going wrong and I didn't like it. When they brought Anne home from the hospital, I locked the front door and threw the key in the commode. Grandma found me in the basement and whooped the daylights out of me.

Henrietta, a more quiet soul, considered Anne to be her girl. Tommie had already put her stamp on me and I was quite unpredictable. Mostly, Henrietta fussed at me for my tomboy ways and tried to make me stop climbing the sycamore tree. It was dangerous, she said. She just could not handle me. She doted on my blonde-haired younger sister. It was not long before I took to roaming the woods and the dead-end road with the older kids.

The Grants, Blacks, Somers, Cooper, and the Aaron families were just folks in Shuffletown. As children, we ran in and out of all the homes and stole cookies from everyone. All families were accepted in our community; we were different, so were the seasons. Winter is white and summer is green.

The Aaron family was almost as white as we were. Their grandmother had been a mix of Cherokee, African and Irish. I remember her photo hanging on Daisy's wall. She had a wild mess of red hair and big green eyes. Her skin was the color of tanned cowhide and she was a beauty. Francis Aaron, her son, knew every plant, tree and vine in the forest and made his own medicines when his kids got sick.

It was an economic thing, us all getting along and living together. We were all farmers and living off the land. In Shuffletown, families had to share the seasons and the wealth or poverty it brought with it. The black families owned their own land and paid taxes too. I did notice that the black folks seemed to walk up and down the road more. In Shuffletown, people were people and kids were kids. Everybody had to work and the kids had chores.

I guess at some horrid time there was a Ku Klux Klan, but no one ever seemed to remember such a group or at least to speak of it. Through good manners and the practice of common decency, that white elephant and the past awfulness of slavery times were ignored. And we made do.

My best friend, Marne, was black. Every day we would grab old boards from dad's granary or the smokehouse to create our playhouse in the grass. We always had to have enough boards to separate the different rooms.

When we were six, they sent us to different schools. There was bigotry I am ashamed of, but when the Mt. Mourne Church burned down, the black families attended Sloan Memorial Presbyterian Church and we all sung hymns in unison. When the new church was built on the dead-end road, they returned to their separate worship and things returned to normal, if you call that normal.

Judy Rozzelle

Jim Crow

We didn't have Jim Crow laws in Shuffletown. I drove the Shuffletown bus to Charlotte for Harrison Rozzelle right as the war ended. I was going to dental college and we left Shuffletown at 7:30 a.m. and returned every day at 5:00 p.m. Except on Saturday, we went to town at 10a.m. and came home at 2 p.m. When the war ended and gas became plentiful again, we lost a lot of riders and Harrison sold the bus to the church.

Nobody had to go to the back of the bus when I was driving it to Charlotte. If a black woman got on with a white child, which one are you going to send to the back? I wasn't going to keep the child up front with me without the woman. Besides, I'd rather talk to adults than children back then.

One of my favorite riders was a black man named George. Sometimes, he stood up front on the bus steps and we talked about everything. First time he rode, he said he wanted to get off near the Cooper house. That is the first house off highway 16 where the local black families have always lived. You turn right onto Old Rozzelles Ferry Road just where William Rozzelle's pasture fence is.

I answered, "Oh, yeah, that's the suburbs of Shuffletown."

Every time after that when he got on the bus he stood up front and talked to me. He was the nicest man; he worked in Charlotte and sometimes when he was paid, he came out to see friends. George was later killed near Mt. Holly. He had gotten off a Greyhound bus in Mt. Holly and was walking towards Shuffletown, probably to catch my bus. It was a Friday, he had probably just been paid, and he told the wrong person. I always felt badly about that.

Dr. Robert Griffin

Work Began At A Young Age

They carried babies to the fields in baskets. When you were old enough to crawl out of the basket, you were old enough to pick cotton. I don't remember anything but hard work; my daddy had many mouths to feed. He was a widower and married three times. He had a passel of us kids. He had kids running around everywhere. Mom took care of Ethel's kids, Minnie Bell's and her own kids.

I was born working. I was so little when Dad taught me how to ride a mule that every morning he had to turn the big old iron pot over so I could stand on it to reach across the mule's back. The pot was what Mom washed clothes in. Yeah, hard work, sturdy people and cotton. That is all I remember about growing up. Well, there was church and singing hymns on the front porch with my family.

Lee Wallace

Basket Babies

They carried babies out into the cotton fields, laid them out on a blanket and shaded them with a basket.

Henrietta Grant Somers

The Gabled House By The Crossroads

Mamie and Esther Gaines lived with their mother, Mrs. Took, in a gabled house tucked in the corner of the crossroads. Their home predated the War of Northern Misunderstanding and was built with pegs instead of nails. The spinsters and their mother were Catholics in a place filled with Methodists and Presbyterians.

I don't have any idea how they arrived in Shuffletown. Mamie and Esther were warm, wonderful women. I believed they were as old as the oak tree that grew in their front yard and if Mrs. Took was their mother, her first husband must have been Methuselah, the oldest man in the Bible. Mrs. Took was so old she had shriveled to the size of a hound dog sitting up. She wore lacy bonnets that covered her face and big white lace collars. She was nice and sweet. However, she did smell like old shoes.

The yard that spread out around their house flourished with exotic plants and trees. Yuccas grew stout and tall beside jade plants, potato vines, wisteria, jonquils and snowball bushes. Little cement Chinese temples sat underneath overgrown bushes. Frogs shared teatime beneath the azaleas.

A statue of St. Francis fed the birds by the cement pond and a golden gazing ball peeked from a tangle of ivy. They could grow any plant from any climate by just sticking it in dirt. Someone brought them a Florida orange tree; they stuck it in a tin washtub in the hallway and for decades the tree grew towards the thin ray of sunlight in the window beside the front door. Faithfully it grew oranges around Christmas that were given to stunned guests. When the guests left, they were invited to look at the goldfish in the deeply dug cement pond in the front yard. The surface of the goldfish pond often froze during the winter but this never seemed to bother the fish.

One winter the surface ice was at least two inches thick, but the goldfish still swam lazily beneath it. The Gaines place was as entertaining as a modern theme park.

Local lore held that long ago, gold treasure was buried somewhere in their yard. The sisters were wise enough to take advantage of this mystery. Several times a year Mamie and Esther became convinced they had a good notion where the gold was buried. They would walk across the road to Mack Gillis' store and tell whoever was standing there that they might find it if they just dug around a little where they told them to. Whoever it was would soon follow them back across the street and take up their shovel. No one ever struck gold, but they sure did get a lot of plants set in the ground.

Judy Rozzelle

Dogtrot House

If you haven't ever seen a dogtrot house, or what we used to call a shotgun house, let me tell you about them. A dogtrot house is built on big rocks or stones set at the four corners and sometimes the rocks are big and high enough that a dog can trot around and under the house. A shotgun house is built with the back door lined up with the front door. If it was necessary, you could stand in the front door and shoot someone running out the back door.

Hank Wallen

Did You Ever Eat Cooter?

Did you ever eat cooters? For you young chaps a cooter is a turtle, a big turtle. My husband used to drive me crazy trying to get me to cook him a cooter. I had to cook him one a couple weeks before he died. He brought one home from visiting his brother. They had caught it up in the country. We used to cook them when I was growing up, but I never ate cooter. Never had any taste for them.

My brothers used to catch them, but I never could eat a cooter. They would go down to the creek or wherever they found them and bring them home in a box. Then they would trick it into sticking its

13

head out and biting a stick they held in front of it. Cooters will not let go once they bite something. When he had a good grip, they would chop his head off.

They got hold of one cooter, chopped its head off and turned it upside down to drain out the stuff inside it. They went back ten hours later, took off the shell and that turtle's heart was still beating.

I do know how to prepare and cook them. You take the shell off and cut the meat away from it. The meat comes out in one big hunk. Then you soak it in water with a teaspoon of salt and vinegar to soak the wild taste out of it. That afternoon you cut it up and fry it like a chicken. The meat tastes like every kind of meat you can imagine. One part will taste like deer; another hunk will taste like chicken or beef. Lord, what we used to eat back then. We were poor but none of us ever went hungry. But when they served turtle, I ate biscuits and honey. Try it if you want to.

Don't let it bite you when you're catching it. And stay away from those feet. They got nails three inches long that can slash a finger off. They remind me of something prehistoric like dinosaurs.

It is good meat; I just can't eat anything that wants to live so bad that its heart keeps beating for that long.

Ivy Aaron Walker

The Big House

Cousin Kissey lived in the big house all her life. She was born there, died there, and we sat with her body for her wake there. She boarded people and fed them three meals a day for more than sixty years. Hers was not an easy life.

There is a photo of the three Rozzelle women, Cousin Kissey, Aunt Anne, her daughter, Betty, an unknown female and a mutt of mixed breed sitting on the back steps of the big house. Days, years of hard labor are scrubbed into each woman's face. It looks like Aunt Anne, a young widow, had already suffered a stroke, but she is smiling. The unknown female isn't too bad looking, but for the past hundred years rumor has told that she was visiting. Let me tell you, the dog was the best looking thing in the picture. The dog probably belonged to the visitor also. I only remember hounds hanging out at Aunt Kissey's porch.

Judy Rozzelle

Cousin Kissey Bakes A Cake

In 1951, Cousin Kissey bought about three dozen eggs or more every other day from Mama Jo and when she called for them, I would take them to her. One time when I walked in the kitchen with the eggs, she was measuring and dumping ingredients in a wooden bowl to make a cake. The bowl was one of the biggest I have ever seen. I mean it was a huge wooden bowl. It was the size of a Volkswagen tire. I bet the bowl was 30 inches across. She set that big old bowl on her hip and commenced to mix the ingredients with her hand. All the time we talked, she was swishing her hand back and forth in that big bowl stirring flour, sugar, eggs and cream until it became a smooth yellow batter. Maybe the human touch was the secret to her cakes?

During those days, Cousin Kissey's restaurant was one of the best places to eat. People still came out from Charlotte, Lincolnton, and even further away to eat dinner there. Eastern Airlines spotlighted the restaurant in a national radio advertisement. Orson Welles was the narrator and I heard one time when he to wait on a plane in Charlotte he came out to the restaurant to eat.

From Thanksgiving until Christmas, the restaurant was reserved every night for private parties. It was a popular place all during the year for family reunions and business parties. And Cousin Kissey never allowed a drop of wine, beer or liquor on the premises. It was one of the last old fashion places to eat and it had been run by the same family for more than one hundred years. I cried when it burned down. All of us did.

Barbara Gillis Rozzelle

Cousin Kissey's Ford Coupe

In 1939, relatives convinced Cousin Kissey to purchase a black Ford coupe. The car became her favorite thing and a constant marvel to her. She parked the car right in front of the house where she used to keep her horse and wagon.

Every morning and each night just before turning in, Cousin Kissey checked on her car. She would pat it and say, "Isn't it a nice car? It's always where you leave it."

Judy Rozzelle

The Night I Was Born

Mary Alice Wallace and me were sitting on the porch one Sunday afternoon. Let's see, I was already an old man so she must have been in her late 80s. I'll never forget that afternoon cause she told me she remembered the night I was born. Both my folks were deaf and she said my daddy, Eddy Wallace, was hard worried that I would be deaf. Dad wasn't born deaf, but he had scarlet fever when he was real young. It left him deaf, but my Mom was born deaf.

"You were born after dark, but it wasn't too late, maybe ten o'clock," Mary Alice said. "After we got you cleaned up and swaddled we called your Dad in to see you. The bedroom was still and all of us were watching Eddie," she said. "He held you for the longest time and without making a sound sister Iris came up behind him and clapped her hands so hard it sounded like a gun going off. You jumped and started to wail."

She said she never again saw a father smile so dearly at a birth than my dad did in that moment.

Mother wanted to keep me in bed with her that first month and she wouldn't let Dad sleep in the bed with her because she was afraid he'd roll over on me. So, he had to sleep on the sofa. Since they were mute, they had to figure out some way for Mom to call him if she needed him in the middle of the night. Every night for the next month, when they went to bed, they tied one end of an old plow line to her wrist and the other end to his wrist before they went to sleep.

Nobody had anything back then, but we could make do.

Lee Wallace

Baby Puddin' Bounces

There are 117 of us Fullers. That includes 29 grandchildren and last I counted 45 great-grandchildren. And it all began with my ten children.

Now as you can imagine, when my kids were young I did not get much rest to speak of. Those were long, hard days for a country woman. Before the sun was up I'd've made a batch of biscuits from scratch, and by the time it'd set I'd've cooked up three big meals for the dozen of us, washed a couple kettles of clothes, put 'em all out to dry, and canned at least half an acre's worth of crops. I had to go to the outhouse just to sit down.

Lots of times after a day on my feet I'd fall to sleep and dream about more of the same: more washin' and cookin'. One night I was washing dishes in my sleep. I had little Puddin' sleeping next to me me and Saul always kept our babies in bed with us until they were old enough to survive sleeping with the bigger kids. Back then, when you finished washing up you threw the dirty water off the back step. So when I finished the dishes in my dream that night, I got out of bed, gathered up what I thought was the dishpan, and tossed the contents outside.

I woke up immediately. "Saul!" I screamed. "THE BABY! I THREW PUDDIN OUT THE WINDOW!"

Everybody came running. But he was all right. He had landed in some bushes, and they broke his fall. He sure did scream, though. After that, I never threw another baby out with the dishwater.

Evelyn Fuller

Mules Are Plain Stubborn

You see that land by the creek; everybody says it is a beautiful place. When I had to plow that field with an old mule all day it didn't look so pretty. When the sun got to the middle of the sky, the heat felt like hell, by that time, your throat was hoarse from hollering at the stubborn hardheaded mule and you were pretty sure that animal was the devil.

I heard of a fella that got so worked up with his mule and he just had to get done with his plowing. It was getting close to dark, he was plowing the last row and the dang mule just stopped pulling the plow. An hour later, the boy was still begging the mule to start up again. Finally, he lit a fire under the mule to get him started again. I know how he felt. Dad sold mules. People tell me, my dad, Eli Wallen, had the strongest and stubbornnest mules around.

Hank Wallen

Mrs. Emma Wilson

Mrs. Emma Wilson was my surrogate grandmother. But she was also my friend, and the first wise woman I ever knew. She liked having me around, and when I went to her house Mother could have some time to herself to sew, paint, or read; she knew I was in good hands.

She did not treat me like a child, but as a peer. I was a sponge, eager to have her tell me stories about how she did things. I loved to watch her churn butter, make biscuits, or hominy. In the winter, I sat by her stove and watched her stoke up the wood fire, or iron with the old flatiron she heated on the woodstove.

I watched her make poke bonnets, mold candles, stir her wash pot, or any other humble chore she undertook. She knew I was a student of life, and she explained everything she did. She had two daughters; but Ruth never married and worked in town. Her other daughter lived in New York and seldom came home. I guess she liked me as her shadow.

Mrs. Wilson's hair was gray and thin, but it hung to her waist when she took it down. I loved to help her comb it, and I loved to watch her get ready for Sundays. She heated water in a kettle, and then washed her hair in a dishpan on the porch. She just used soap, then poured lemon juice on it to take off the soap scum. Then she'd lean over the porch rail and comb it out in the sun. She would fluff it, comb it again, and in no time, it was dry enough to style. I would follow her into her bedroom where she'd sit on a stool before her mirror. She parted her hair in the middle, then made more parts down each side, and tied the sections off with pieces of string. Then she'd take about two inches of the sectioned hair, and make a long thin braid. She wound loose hair from her comb around the end, and worked her way up and around the sections. When her hair was all braided, she would wrap each braid around a twig, and tie it with a piece of white rag. She would wear this bizarre headwear all day. When she and Mr. Larry got into their Model T Ford to go to Shuffletown Grocery, she would put her poke bonnet over it.

Next morning, she would remove the rags, and twigs, unbraid her hair and comb it. She had perfect little Lady Godiva waves. She would fasten it into a bun at the nape of her neck, then put on her serviceable little thirties hat, and pull the rubber band under her bun to hold it in place. The rest of her outfit usually consisted of a navy blue dress with white collar, dark cotton stockings, lace up shoes, and a sensible little purse. Of course, she also wore white gloves for church.

Her only makeup was a little face powder, lipstick and rouge, and she usually wore her pearl earbobs that Mr. Larry had given her when they were engaged.

I cannot think of my childhood without remembering her. I am grateful she was in my life.

Gail E. Haley

I Was The Last Born Of Eight Children

Families were big back then and each child was born to help on the farm. It was cheap labor. My parents thought they had had all the children they needed when they moved into the big house just off Mt. Holly Huntersville Road. The house has a big wraparound porch and in those days, wide-open fields just right for livestock and crops surrounded it. But there was also a railroad track at the end of the property and a train rolled across those tracks several times a day.

The first train ran early in the morning and blew its whistle loud and clear. I don't know what time it ran, but I remember Poppa telling me the train always woke up him and Momma. He said it was too early to get up and too late to go back to sleep. I was born nine months later just as the morning train whistled. I have always been fond of whistling trains. It tells me someone has just arrived.

Wallace Innis

Growing Up Country

Exotic Places

There wasn't an inch of land throughout Shuffletown we didn't know by heart. Our world was the same as the adults, yet very different. Our land was filled with exotic places, danger and adventure. Each day we stalked wild creatures, defended our homesteads, tracked cattle rustlers and panned for gold by the edge of the pond.

Indians stampeded buffalo in Uncle Harrison's pasture and cowboys camped by Dad's pond. The forbidden swamp marked the land behind Shuffletown Grocery. Behind the store were two acres of flat land where Uncle Tad had dynamited five minnow ponds. They were small ponds. Each pond was only a little larger than a two-car garage. When we tired of the adventurous life, we'd sit in the ditch across the road and watch as Uncle Tad and Cousin Eddie, both wearing hip boots, seined in the muddy water for minnows to sell at the store.

When the corn grew tall in the fields, the path to King Solomon's mines unfolded for us. Between the rows of long-leafed cornstalks poisonous snakes hung from trees, crocodiles slept in the sun along riverbanks and fierce red-plumed Zulus waited for us.

It was the far right-hand corner of my father's cornfield, and it was thousands of miles away from home.

Judy Rozzelle

Huckleberry Summers

Our house faced what Aunt Judy calls the dead-end road. I could look out my bedroom window and see the old barn and great big old oak trees. It was a wonderful sight. We used to swim in the old Long Creek swimming hole. We'd ride our bikes to the creek and swim unsupervised. There were no houses around the creek back then, and that water was clean. We loved to play in that creek. Somebody built a dam across the creek and made a good-sized pond. It was alive with turtles, frogs and crawdads. The water smelled...alive. The rocks were always slippery and so were the frogs. Looking back it seems like a dream or a scene from an old Mark Twain book.

We loved to fish for bass and brim. We'd hook some big fish especially brim. A good-sized brim puts up a good fight. Lots of times we'd reel in a fish only to realize it was a "shiner." Fishermen sometimes dumped their minnow buckets into the pond when they finished fishing, and the minnows would grow to a good size, and they would take our bait. Most of our time was spent getting our lines untangled from tree limbs and stumps.

The younger kids had an especially hard time keeping their lines free. The older kids would laugh at the younger ones, and sometimes give them a hand getting untangled.

William (Bill) Alexander Rozzelle IV

Dad Still Gets Mad

Come to think of it. There are two things I did fifty years ago that still make Dad mad today. He still gets mad about Scout's finger, but, heck, Scout is a doctor. I don't think he is a surgeon but he is a doctor. And it was just the top of the finger.

The other thing that makes him mad is when he remembers the time I was trying to help him wash his new car...he thought I had a rag, but I had a hammer.

He was scrubbing the rear of the car and I swear he said, "Go ahead," when I asked if his headlights needed smashing.

I smashed the front headlight. Then I hit the other with the hammer.

Dad looked like a raging bull when he got to me. He whooped the daylights out of me.

Rob Griffin

Raising Rob Griffin

When I was pregnant with him, every time I sat down, he stood up. He was born with his pants on fire. The first thing he did after he learned to walk was run away from home. He had on nothing but a diaper. I looked and looked. Finally, I ran to the neighbors and had everybody looking for Rob. We were combing the woods when I saw Amos Huffstone carrying him down the road from the direction of Shuffletown.

Rob walked away all the time. I caught him going down the driveway so many times, I could not keep up with him. I finally bought a dog leash and hooked it around him when I had to go to town.

21

What else could I do? I felt badly about the leash being so short, but I knew where he was. I could not chase him down the driveway all day. I had work to do so I attached a rope to it and tied him to the clothesline. It was the practical thing to do. I often tethered the cow close to Rob to keep him entertained. The cow seemed not to mind. Oh, it might have aggravated the cow when Rob pried open the cow's mouth and stuck his head inside. He just couldn't figure out how the cow ate grass or why? I have a photo of that somewhere.

Mrs.Susan Griffin

On Running Away

It was so dry the day I ran away I thought I was going to choke to death on that road when Andy Huffstone brought me home. She tied me to a fence like I was a junkyard dog. Yeah, I remember all that. I don't care if I was real young.

Rob Griffin

The Axe

Oh, the boys were watching me sharpen the axe. When I finished, I hung the axe up and told the boys not to touch it. I should have just given it to them to save them the trouble of getting it. From what they told me, they had the axe before I got out of sight. Rob got a stick, put it down on the ground, and was trying to chop it into two pieces. His brother Scout was anxious for his turn, but Rob's stick could not chop his stick in two. Scout wanted to move the stick, but Rob told him that if he touched the stick he would chop his finger off. Rob has always meant what he said and when Scout touched the stick, Rob chopped his finger.

Scout came flying in the back door with his finger bleeding and I went flying outside and grabbed Rob. That was the first time I paddled him. Rachel wrapped a towel around Scout's finger and we rushed him to Dr. Moore in Mt. Holly. Poor Scout, he just bled and bled. I took them inside to Dr. Moore, came back outside, and paddled Rob again. I paddled Rob about four times that day. I think Rachel paddled him a couple of times.

Dr. Robert Griffin

22

They Paddled Me, Again And Again

My parents paddled me every time they thought about it for the next month. This is what really happened. Scout and I watched Dad sharpen his axe. When Dad walked away he said, "Boys, don't touch the axe." That was an invitation to trouble. We couldn't wait to get hold of it. Quick as Dad went inside, we scrambled into the shed and got it from where he had hung it up. I got there first, so the axe was mine. I drug it outside and found a stick about a yard long. I placed it on the ground and the ground was a little soft, but I kept swinging at that stick.

Finally, Scout, he was the brainy one, said let's take it to a harder place and chop it there. I didn't want him telling me what to do. He kept saying it. I said no, now go away. Then he said he was going to pick it up and chop it himself. I told him at least three times not to touch my stick. The last time, I added that if he touched my stick I would chop his finger off. Well, he touched it and I did what I told him I would do. Scout ran screaming to the house, I ran to the shed to put the axe up, that's where Dad got hold of me, and he paddled the daylights out of me.

I rode in the backseat on the way to Mt. Holly. I was crying and saying I was sorry. They told me to stay in the car. After they got inside Dad came out to the car, yanked me out, wore me out again, then he took me in the doctor's office. Then he wore me out when we left the doctor's office. When we got home, Mother took over and she paddled me. I got a paddling and a lecture every time they thought about it for a month after that. I really came to regret that move. The only thing I ever did to Scout after that was make him swallow pennies.

Rob Griffin

Rob Falls In The Outhouse Hole

Rob fell in the outhouse hole the very day we installed indoor plumbing. Dr. Griffin was moving the outhouse so he could cover up the hole. Rob was curious and wanted to help. Rob was pushing one end of the outhouse, I heard his father hollering, and when I looked out the window, Rob had fallen in the hole.

His father pulled him out with the rake handle and told him to get to the house. Oh, no, Rob was not coming in my house like that. I was going to keep him, but I was going to wash him off outside. I poured buckets of water on him to get him clean enough to bring inside to bathe.

Mrs. Susan Griffin

She Scrubbed Me Raw

Mother came outside and stripped me down. Then she washed me off with cold water, scrubbed me with lye soap and a brush…and then brought me inside so she could scrub me more. I felt like I had sunburn for two weeks.

Rob Griffin

Picking Blackberries

There were a couple of drawbacks to picking blackberries. If a snake didn't bite you, the chiggers would eat you up.

The night before we were going blackberry picking Mother would get the kerosene and put a drop of it on a teaspoon of sugar and give it to each one of us. I remember watching her lift the wick out of the kerosene lamp and letting a drop of kerosene spill on a teaspoon of sugar. We'd line up for our chigger medicine. The kerosene was supposed to keep chiggers off you. If she didn't have kerosene, she would use a drop of spirits of turpentine. The next morning she would have us rub kerosene on our ankles and wrists. By the time the sun was over the corncrib, our bare feet were running down the footpath towards the blackberry bushes.

One time I stepped on a snake with my bare feet. His body was as cold as it could be. Long after I stopped screaming, I could still feel my foot on that cold rubbery body. By noon, we were home with our pails filled with juicy blackberries. And despite the kerosene, I always had chigger bites.

Mother used kerosene for a lot of things. If Father got sore from plowing or blacksmithing, she would put a drop of kerosene or spirits of turpentine on a teaspoon of sugar. He said it made the soreness go away.

Ivy Aaron Barnes

Thumbsucking Cured

Did Mom tell you about stopping Scout and me from sucking our thumbs? Well, we were thumb suckers and when we were about three and four years old, she decided that she had had enough of our thumb sucking.

She bought some of that stuff to stop kids from sucking their thumbs, every night she would paint our thumbs, and we hated it. It burned our thumbs and tasted horrible. One day when Scout and I were supposed to be taking a nap, I suggested that we go downstairs and pour the stuff out. We did. We sneaked downstairs real quiet like and got the bottle, went outside and poured it out.

When it was empty, Scout, the thinker, asked what we were going to fill it with to keep her from knowing it was gone. The stuff was yellow and we couldn't think of anything. I truly do not remember whose idea it was, but we decided to pee in the bottle. We sat it on the ground and made a game out of it. When it was full, we put it back and went back to our beds.

That night when it was bedtime, Mom came upstairs and asked us to hold out our thumbs. Then it dawned on us what we had done. We screamed and hollered, then we confessed, but she painted our thumbs anyhow, cut off the light and left the room. That was the night we stopped sucking our thumbs.

Rob Griffin

Chickens

When I was growing up, we always had chickens. There were a hundred or more of them, red feathered, short tempered, squawking chickens. I tormented them in many ways. One afternoon, I decided I would play schoolhouse with them. In order to do this I considered it necessary to begin by getting all of them inside the chicken house to call the roll. That must have been some sight. One hundred chickens going in one hundred directions. I was hollering, stomping, and schussing them towards the chicken house. It was like trying to catch water with a sieve. They flew. They ran. They retreated under the hen house. They ran for the barn. They flew into dad's peach trees. Some ran in circles. Others headed out across the pasture. I sat down and laughed at the frenzy. However, the squawking and mayhem brought mother to the back steps. Even the chickens snapped to attention when she hollered, "Judy Elizabeth!"

That game was over. Dad said he lost about twenty hens that day to heart failure. They were laying eggs again in about a week and I was allowed to go outside and play. Mother often stood at the back steps until I had cleared the chicken yard.

Feeding the chickens was my afternoon chore. I was supposed to stand in the middle of the chicken yard and toss handfuls of cracked corn into the yard while the chickens ran about pecking at the ground, fighting for the corn. This approach to feeding took entirely too long.

I did it correctly once and it seemed like two days. Then I discovered that if I just poured the corn in a line on the ground the chore was over quicker and the chickens seemed to like it. Some days I poured corn in a straight line. Some days I made circles with the corn. Some days I made short parallel lines. One day I poured a line leading into the chicken house. I never did figure out how to get them to line up for their rations.

Every spring Dad ordered boxes of brand new chicks. They always arrived when spring mornings were still cold. The world was so new to them. Each chick was nothing more than a fistful of feathers and a beak. They were always scared and confused. They were also stupid. They drowned in their water troughs. They suffocated in piles. A little more than half always survived. Anne loved it each year when they arrived. I always thought they were sad, like children snatched from their mom too soon. I rarely visited the chicken coop where they were kept under bright lights.

And I have never been able to erase the sight of Henrietta and Momma wringing a chicken's neck from the images in my mind. To wring a chicken's neck you grab them by the head, twist, and the neck stretches and the chicken squawks until it's all over. I just don't know how it is humanely possible to kill an animal like that, but I never did go hungry either. It wasn't much better when Henrietta would run a chicken down, hold it down on an old stump and chop its head off with a sharp axe. Either way, the chicken's headless body circled about in the yard for about five minutes, unaware that it was dead.

The best time between the chickens and me was when I was learning to drive a car. Some time in my fifteenth year, Mom decided that if I was going to learn to drive, I would have to teach myself; she sure wasn't getting in a car with me at the wheel. After school, when I had eaten my snacks and fidgeted and begged until I was about to drive her crazy, she would go to her pocketbook and take out the car keys and hold them out to me and say, "Judy, if you run over a cow or run the car through a building or hit the garage, one of us will have to leave home; and you can't cook."

I would snatch the keys, head for the door, and as I was opening the car door, she always came to the screen and hollered, "Don't run over any chickens, either." She would shake her head and go back to her sewing.

I'd jump in the old blue Plymouth, spark the engine; rev the motor and circle around the low pump house in the front yard. Then I'd drive down to the garage, turn around and come flying back up the driveway, around the front of the house, hang a left, shift into third gear and head towards the chicken yard. The chickens would hear me coming and head for the hen house. Dad sold the chickens before I turned sixteen.

Judy Rozzelle

Baseball

If we wanted to play baseball, we rounded up a bunch of kids, walked off the bases and chose sides. We would go to Mr. Gillis's store and buy a baseball. If somebody hit the ball out of bounds into the woods, we'd have to stop the game until we found it. We'd argue over bad calls the big kids were always right.

Several mornings I'd be awakened by one of the kids insisting that I come play ball, and they didn't take no for an answer. We played basketball year round. We shot baskets beside the barn, played pick-up games, and challenged each other to games of "horse." Apples were in abundance everywhere. When we finished playing a game, we'd eat those apples, but mostly we threw them at each other. One day we learned that if you took a long, flexible stick and stuck an apple on the end of it, you could fling that apple a long, long way. We flung apples all over the place, until we got yelled at for wasting apples.

William (Bill) Rozzelle IV

Girls In Overalls

When I was growing up in Shuffletown, my daddy had a molasses mill and people from all around the county would bring cane for him to make their molasses. We also grew cane in our fields. The cane had tough stalks. When the cane was ready to cut, we had to take the fodder off and cut the cane down. As you cut the stalks, you stacked it into piles. In due time someone would bring the mule and wagon around and we would load the crop to take it to the mill across Rozzelle Ferry Road over near where Will Sr. and Emma Lynn Rozzelle lived.

Inside the mill, there was a pole and you hooked the mule to it. The mule walked in circles and we would poke the stout jointed stalks in the millstone. The light-colored syrup ran out into a tub. When we were through, Daddy poured the syrup into an eight-foot-long pan that was divided into three sections. A fire was lit under the pan and the process of boiling down the syrup began. The juice of the sugar cane was boiled in each section. As Daddy poured it from section one

27

to section two, and finally, to section three, the syrup turned from a golden brown juice to the best molasses in the county.

We were a family of five kids and everyone worked. There were three girls and two boys, Mable, Carl, me, Connor and Ollie. If there was something that needed doing whether it was plowing or planting the girls worked just like the boys. One day, Fred Wallen, our neighbor, asked Daddy, "don't you wish these big strapping girls was boys?"

"Well, no, Fred, I don't," answered Daddy. "I wish the boys were girls."

Fred and other neighbors often came over to watch the molasses making. One day Fred brought his son, John Mack, with him and John asked in a loud voice, "Daddy, is Maria a boy or girl?" That is because I wore overalls all the time and he could not tell if I was a boy or girl. I don't know why, because Mama always made us put on a bonnet when we were outside. She was determined to protect our complexions. Ollie had to sleep in her bonnet for a week once when Momma caught her outside without it on her head.

I remember when there were no yards to mow. We did not have to mow grass because when we saw a sprig of grass in the yard we'd dig it up with a hoe. The grass only grew up to a certain point. We swept our yard and kept it clean. I clearly remember Mama sweeping the yard. All the women swept their yards back then and everyone had a nice clean yard and no one mowed grass. We didn't have time; anyhow, farming took all day.

Back then our address had a route number and our mailboxes had a box number. But the name of the road has always been Rozzelle Ferry Road. They have changed the name from Rozzelle Ferry to Belhaven up past the crossroads of Mt. Holly Huntersville Road at Shuffletown. I hope they never change the name down our way. Today we all watch as they are clearing trees and rocks with huge bulldozers on land that once belonged to Tad Rozzelle. Developers are making room for housing developments and businesses. It is very sad to watch bulldozers push away life as we knew it. I can remember when there were only five houses in the two-mile stretch from Rozzelle Ferry Bridge to the crossroads at Shuffletown. Soon, it will be hard to imagine how we once lived as farmers on this land.

Maria Hooper

My First Wedding

I ran behind my brother as he skirted rifle fire and serpentines through the woods, ducking with him behind rocks and trees as he returned fire and hollered, "*Poppoppoppoppop.*"

It was the sound of terror and I kept my head down until he ran again. They were playing war and I remember that crystalline day under a clear blue sky. Soon I began to discover my own hideouts, my own imaginary evil and magic. It was my turn.

I was long-legged and gangly. I got married for the first time during those days. Over my blue jeans and shirt, I wore a white curtain and carried flowers from mother's white hydrangea bush. The bridesmaids wore an assortment of clothing, but their hats were flowers and leaves. The groom was in a hurry 'cause we had the west to settle and Indians were waiting by the pond. My "husband" and I killed the bad guys and rustlers until our mothers called us home. It was my best attempt at matrimony.

Judy Rozzelle

The Mailman Rides A Bull

I was a kid and someone dared me. For the most part, Joseph was a peaceable old bull, and I thought, "Why not?" I was going to be the first mailman to deliver mail in these parts, and I thought that the sight of a redheaded mailman riding a black bull would be something to see.

When I got the job at fourteen, I saddled up Joseph and we rode over to the post office in Paw Creek, picked up the mail and delivered it to about fifteen families in Shuffletown.

Joseph was big and wide. It was like riding a big old rocking chair. We were never in a hurry we just clopped along in and out of the ruts on the washboard roads. After a couple of years, I started using Pop's buckboard and gave Joseph the rest he deserved. but yeah, you heard right. Joseph and I got the mail out. We were quite a team. And it was fun at the time.

Mac Gillis

The Lord's Prayer

The whole time I was growing up at home and anytime I visited thereafter, I gathered with my family to pray in the den. It was always just after Dad had watched the evening news. Mom set down her sewing.

29

Dad folded the newspaper. My sister and I slipped from our places on the couch to our knees, we bowed our heads and Daddy prayed.

"Dear God, we come before you to give thanks. We are grateful to you for bringing us back together tonight and thanks for watching over us as we go our different ways each day. Be with us, comfort and guide us."

These words were spoken each night. Dad followed the preamble with prayer requests that changed according to the amount of the day's gratitudes and needs. He prayed for rain. He prayed for the crops. He prayed for the sick and our neighbors. He prayed for our continued health. His opening was short and focused. He led us to the grand finale when we all spoke in unison reciting *the Lord's Prayer.* Dad led the prayer. His voice was steady and sure.

"Our Father which art in Heaven," he began, "Hallowed be thy Name." He recited the complete prayer. I listened for him to come to my favorite phrases, "Lead us not into Temptation. Deliver us from Evil. For Thine is the Kingdom, the Power and the Glory. Amen."

I was alert by the time he spoke these words. Temptation was already giving me a lot of trouble even back then. And I believed in ghosts as surely as an anchor sits on the ocean floor. I waited for the verses about temptation and delivering us from evil, and my voice was steady and pleading when I spoke these words. When the prayer was finished, I could go to bed and hope to sleep knowing God had detained evil.

Judy Rozzelle

Mama Jo's Kitchen

When I was a kid, I loved to be with Mama Jo almost more than I loved my own mama. When I got home from school, I dropped off my books at the house and headed for Mama Jo's. There were two places in the house I would find her. Either she would be bent over her sewing machine making a dress or she would be in the kitchen.

My absolutely favorite place to be with Mama Jo was the kitchen. My two aunts, Judy and Anne, were always popping in and out. If they were going to stay a while, they would jump up on the washing machine and talk to us.

Aunt Judy was the wacky aunt and I never knew what to expect from her. One time she came in for a Coca Cola and when she popped off the top the rim of the bottle was chipped. Mama Jo said she couldn't drink it because of the chip. That was when Cokes were a treat. Mama

Jo bought a carton of six bottles when she made her once-a- week trip to the grocery store. For a minute, Aunt Judy was stumped, but soon she pulled open a drawer, pulled out a thin tea towel, and strained the Coke into a glass.

Aunt Anne was always coming into the kitchen taking a couple of slices of bread. Then she would roll them into little balls and eat them while sitting on the washing machine.

When Mama Jo was going to make stickies, she would slide out the board that was built in above the drawers in her cabinets. Mama Jo told Uncle Houston when the house was being built exactly how to she wanted her cabinets, and her directions included a board that could be pulled out for rolling out cookies, biscuits and stickies. When she finished, she cleaned the board and slid it out of sight until the next time. I can still see Mama Jo pulling out that board, flouring it, placing a mound of kneaded dough on it and wheeling her rolling pin across it until it was just right.

To make stickies Mama Jo rolled out the dough until it was almost thin as paper. Then she would smear Mrs. Filbert's butter with a spatula. Then she would cover the dough with brown sugar, raisins, and pecans. When she was finished, she would roll up the dough and slice it into stickies. Sometimes the nuts and raisins would push through the thin dough and crack it open in spots. Because the dough was so thin, she had to be careful not to burn them when they were baked. Sometimes she did but a few, but no matter how hard a sticky it was. they were all eaten. Perfectly cooked stickies were sticky and gooey from the butter and the sugar. When they stuck together and you pulled them apart there was always a trailing sweet caramel string.

When she finished, her apron and her hands were always covered with flour. Mama Jo was an alchemist. In her kitchen, she turned flour into love.

Barbara (Babs) Rozzelle Wiley

Stickies

1 box Pillsbury Hot Roll Mix
1 stick margarine
1 cup brown sugar (packed)
2 teaspoons cinnamon
1 cup chopped pecans

Mix dough from one box Pillsbury Hot Roll Mix according to package directions. After dough has risen, divide it in half for two makings. Roll one ball of dough to ⅛ inch thickness. Spread evenly with ½ stick of margarine. Sprinkle with ½ cup of brown sugar (packed), one teaspoon cinnamon and ½ cup of chopped pecans. Roll in jelly roll fashion and cut in one inch slices. Place the slices on a well buttered sheet pan so that they are not touching and let stand for one hour. Place them in a preheated 375° oven until golden brown. Repeat recipe with second half of the dough.

If desired, cover the unbaked stickies with aluminum foil and place in the freezer. For future use as a convenient snack. When removed from freezer, allow them to stand 2 hours before baking.

Mama Jo's Stickies

1 box Pillsbury Hot Roll Mix
One stick margarine
One cup brown sugar (packed)
2 teaspoons cinnamon
1 cup chopped pecans

Mix dough from one box Pillsbury Hot Roll Mix according to package directions. After dough has risen, divide it in half for two batches of stickies.

Roll one ball of dough to 1/8-inch thickness. Spread evenly with ½ stick of margarine. Spread with ½ cup of brown sugar (packed), one teaspoon cinnamon and ½ cup of chopped pecans. Roll in jellyroll fashion and cut in one inch slices. Place the stickies on a well buttered sheet pan so that they are not touching and let stand for one hour.

After an hour, place them in a preheated 375-degree oven until golden brown. Repeat recipe with second half of the dough.

If desired, cover the unbaked stickies with aluminum foil and place in the freezer to be baked later. When you remove them from the freezer, allow them to stand an hour before baking.

Pet Cemetery

In a forgotten shady corner by the pond was the cemetery for family pets. My dog Skipper rests there, along with my mixed cocker spaniel, Whiskey, Will's dog, Snookie, and Twist, my sister's dog.

They were all strays that wandered up to the back porch hungry. They never slept inside the house, but they were fed and loved. They ran beside us wherever we wandered. In return, we shared our treats with them, tossed them sticks, and picked fat swollen ticks out of their fur.

When each died, we wept buckets of tears and swore never to forget them. Their burial was always a ritual. Dad carried them to the pond, laid them on the ground, and dug a deep hole. Then he would lay them gently in their grave and begin to fill the hole. As hard as it was, we stood by until the deed was done. We uttered a prayer, then said "Goodbye" to our faithful companions.

Dad held our hands as we walked up the hill without a dog at our heels.

Judy Rozzelle

Cows

Few people today understand how once our very lives were tied to the ways of the earth and its animals. They only know milk comes in a plastic container. There are few of us left who share the memory of a lumbering cow coming towards the barn, her breath sweet with hay and grass, much less the feel of the fullness of her belly or her short wiry fur.

They were uncomplicated animals and part of the natural order of things. A cow and her owner had a symbiotic relationship. The cow supplied the farmer with milk, butter, cheese and buttermilk. In return, the farmer fed her, gave her shelter, and milked her twice daily. Her milk does not flow until she has a calf. This is when a cow "comes fresh," an old country saying. It there is a drought; her milk may dry up from lack of moisture.

The farmer's kids had to be sure that the cow did not eat wild onions. If she did, the milk would taste of onions for days. One family, during a late summer drought in which their well went dry, fed their cow buckets of blackberries. Her milk became an eerie, blue purple color, but it sustained the family and the cow until a new well could be dug.

The sound of a cowbell in late afternoon signaled that Bessie was coming to the barn to be milked. You knew without looking, she was stepping quickly almost pulling herself forward with the movement of her head, and her belly was swaying, side to side, but she stopped to eat a tempting clump of green grass. So you always had to go and fetch her.

Gail E. Haley

Guinea Hens

I kept guinea hens. You could eat the eggs and at night, they roosted in the tree out front. I tell you this for sure. Nothing can sneak up on a tree full of guinea hens. They holler like dogs if someone surprises them and there is no way to calm down a tree full of hollering hens. They don't care anything about bones. The big hens squawk. It sounds like they are hollering, *Pot Raaack, Pot Raaack, Pot Raack.* It is truly an awful sound, but you know you're safe as long as there's quiet.

And I tell you right now that none of my kids could sneak inside past curfew without rousing those hens. Those hens were a security alarm. And the little biddies were so dear at night; their call sounded like they were saying, *Put away, put away,* like they are ready to get in their little house. The biddies have to be put up until they can fly to keep foxes from getting them. Well, most everything ate little biddies so I gathered them up every night and placed them in a little house.

Pop (Saul) Fuller

Camping On The Pond

When I was thirteen or fourteen, Rupp and I used to think it was a blast to camp out on the banks of Pop-Pop's pond. After supper, we'd go to Shuffletown Grocery and blow our change on junk food and head to the pond. We'd set up my old green Boy Scout tent between two trees on the crest of a hill and gather up wood for a fire. Then we'd sit by the water and watch dragonflies dart among the cattails, throw rocks at the turtles in the pond and look for the spiders that walk on water like it's glass. There was always something to do at the pond and it was a good place to talk trash. We'd pick a target and play tiddlywinks with our knives. As it got dark, we'd light the fire and talk more trash and tell ghost stories. It got real quiet on the pond when it got real dark. At first, you could hear fish jumping and the bullfrogs call to each other; the later it got the quieter you could hear. I haven't heard a quiet like that since. In the movies this is when monsters and psychopaths watch the unsuspecting from the edge of the black night. It was just the campfire, the darkness and us. The world seemed far away. On windy nights when the trees swayed and their branches brushed against each other, you could get nervous about the situation. One particular night a storm was blowing in, the skies darkened early and the trees were swaying in the wind. When the sky rumbled and lightning cracked through the night, we crawled in the tent and fell asleep listening to the rain on the tent. Sometime around midnight, the tent poles started shaking, a head popped through the tent flap and a flashlight beam fell on our faces. We screamed loud enough for us to be heard in town. It was Pop-Pop. He always came down to check on us when we camped on the pond. Pop-Pop looked into the tent and said, "Didn't mean to scare you boys. You doing all right?"

We had been doing fine. But he had just scared us out of a year's growth. Nothing has scared me like that since then. I didn't get that scared when I was a member of a Coast Guard helicopter search and rescue team in Alaska. I always tried to stay awake until after his visit, but I never made it. We didn't need to tell ghost stories, we had Pop-Pop to scare us senseless.

Bob Bradley

35

The School Bus

After you learn to read, add, subtract and multiply, it is not all play and homework. First, you have to survive the ride home. It is the school bus that teaches you the true meaning of the Darwin Theory, survival of the fittest.

The school bus is an orange mobile universe that terrifies parents, teachers and most bus drivers. In this universe, David is required to face Goliath five days a week. Like childbirth and blows to the head, the memory of the experience recedes with time.

The rear view mirrors were smaller on buses in my day. This was good in that the bus driver's sight was restricted; unlike teachers, drivers did not have eyes in the back of the head. Therefore, we could use books as weapons and pocketknives to write on metal. It was a creative atmosphere racked with screams and crying.

Cousin Yvonne, to this day, attributes the many times I hit her on the head with my history book to her headaches. She also attributes my wackiness to the many times she hit me over the head with her history book.

Amid this maddening throng, high-pitched discussions among the kids included threats of fistfights between fathers and references to mothers who wore combat boots. Comic books were currency.

It was Gail Haley's choice of reading material on the school bus that astonished me as much as the fact that she played the marimba. And she played it in public. After boarding the school bus, Gail would retrieve from her red school satchel the latest issue of the *Reader's Digest* to peruse. And you know what she read? She read the section that was entitled *Towards a More Picturesque Speech*. You don't pick on a kid who reads such stuff. You just tuck your book under your arm and walk away shaking your head and thanking God that you were not born unbalanced.

Judy Rozzelle

Bikes

Everybody had an old bike. It was our basic transportation to anywhere and everywhere we wanted to go. They were also entertainment. We'd rebuild them, do stunts with them—pulling wheelies was our favorite. Once we built a ramp at the bottom of a long downhill driveway. Then we would watch while the braver or dumber ones of us jumped the ditch at the end of that ramp. One guy's handlebars broke off, from doing so many wheelies, but he still jumped the ditch with no handlebars.

Frank Rozzelle

The Paperboys

They came in late summer, just before the beginning of school. I must have been nine or ten years old. The pond was new then and it was a great place for bonfires and roasting hotdogs. They were paperboys. Many of them helped support their families with their afternoon paper routes. They were a shy and suspicious lot. Dad had them picked up at all points of the county and brought to our place for an evening of fishing, touch football and a weenie roast.

I can still see that big blazing orange fire and all those straightened clothes hangers, skewered with hotdogs, swinging in the orange flames. Dad built the fire from scratch with tree limbs and firewood. Mom brought the food and the wire coat hangers. Desert always included roasting marshmallows.

It was one of those late summer afternoons when the sun was low in the sky and golden rays fell across the land like long fingers that I played my last touch football game. While we were waiting on all the boys to arrive, dad counted out teams for football in the side yard beside the red wooden shed where he parked his cars and the Farm All tractor. That afternoon there were nine boys and me. Dad and Willie Campbell were dividing up the teams, without me, the teams would have been an uneven number. I was leaning against the garage watching with the football tucked under my arm. Dad finally looked my way, grinned and motioned me over to the team of four. I was wearing blue jeans and a red-checkered shirt. I'm sure that, as usual, I was chewing bubble gum and there was probably a remnant of a pink bubble somewhere in my bangs.

I was a tomboy and proud of it. Girls had to wear dresses to grade school back then, but I always wore my jeans under my dresses. I'd roll them up until I got out of the house. When I reached the big oak tree in front of Mrs. Took's house, I'd stomp my foot until the jeans shook down. Then I'd unroll them the rest of the way and run to the bus stop. It didn't bother me when Cousin Yvonne laughed. She was a sissy. I was tall, skinny and awkward, but I could run with a football and shoot a basketball, that's what counted.

I don't recall much about that specific game of tag football. It was the usual running, catching, falling and scoring. I don't recall who won or how many games we played. But as dusk was spreading across the field and we were walking to the pond, I overheard a bunch of boys talking. I do not remember the exact words, but I could show you the spot I was standing on in the pasture when I heard them say something about me being a girl and they wouldn't play with me again.

My cousins, all the other kids and I played tag football almost every day. They never said anything about me being different. Those games were always games of wild abandon that included running, screaming and pushing. It never bothered any of us whether or not I was at the bottom of the pile or the last one to jump on top of the piled bodies. I had even given a couple of them a black eye. When that happened, Mom called me inside and do some chore like help Henrietta cut up chickens for frying or worse, iron.

It had never once occurred to any of us that I was a girl or that made me any different. For the first time, I knew I was doing something girls weren't supposed to do. Later, I climbed a tree and watched the boys gathered around the fire, and wondered if any one of them could outrun me.

Judy Rozzelle

The Runaway Boat

Mom and Dad both worked. In the summer time, we were free as birds. Like Tom Sawyer and Huckleberry Finn, we lived outdoors and rode our bikes everywhere. Bikes were entertainment. We'd rebuild them, do stunts with them. Pulling wheelies for distance was our favorite challenge.

When we got older and I had my driver's license, Dad's boat became a source for an afternoon of fun. Frank, Babs and I would hitch the boat and trailer to the car and head to the river to ski. We had a powerful craving to ski. There was no harm done if we made it back home and had the boat in place before Mom and Dad came in from work.

It was a blue and white 18 foot boat with a 75 horsepower Johnson outboard motor. It was Dad's boat and he liked it a lot. We hadn't had it that long. It could reach speeds up to 30 mph pulling two skiers.

One day, we decided to leave early to have more time to ski. We ran around grabbing the snacks and soda. When the cooler was in the car, Babs ran back in to put a roast on to cook for supper while Frank and I hitched up the boat. This was something we did a couple of times a week, we had the routine perfected, except on this day. Babs always rode in the back seat and Frank rode shotgun. The river was about a mile away, but Shuffletown crossroads was only about three blocks from our driveway. I turned left at the crossroads and about the time I drove by Shuffletown Grocery, a boat pulled alongside the car.

Babs saw it first. "Look, we're being passed by a boat."

Frank looked at me and said, "Where'd that boat come from?" He looked out the rear window and all he said was, "Damn."

I looked out the window and hollered, "That's Dad's boat." I whipped the car into the parking lot at the grill and we all jumped out to see where the boat was going. Somebody must've noticed it when it passed the grocery cause Uncle Tad and several others came out to look. I just knew it was going to hit a car head on and hurt somebody.

Frank kept saying, "You were supposed to put the pin in the hitch. That's your job." Babs was laughing and hooting. Dad would never hit a girl, but at that moment, I wanted to.

The boat rolled on down the road and all eyes were on it. I figured this was our last day on earth. Suddenly, as if the rudder had been turned, the boat drifted off the road and began to role down the hill towards Uncle Tad's minnow ponds. It rolled and rolled until the trailer hit a rock and the boat became airborne and splashed into a minnow pond. I couldn't believe what I saw. All of us breathed a sight of relief. I heard Frank say, "Good God?"

Then they all noticed us standing in the grill parking lot in our swimsuits. Uncle Tad hollered over that he didn't allow skiing in his minnow ponds. Eddie added that we had to throw back every minnow we caught if we were going to fish. It was not our finest hour.

I drove the car down to the ponds while Frank and Babs ran ahead to retrieve the boat. This time we remembered to place the pin in the hitch.

We spent most of the day putting our story together. Finally, we decided to throw ourselves on Dad's mercy, after we told him it was the first time we'd ever tried this and we certainly would never do it again. I don't remember what happened, but it would have been much worse, except that Dad had almost sunk the boat the previous weekend because he had forgotten to plug the deck of the boat. We waited awhile before we went skiing again.

William (Bill) Alexander Rozzelle IV

The Farm All Tractor

The first thing I ever drove was the ever-faithful Farm All Tractor. I don't think Daddy every bothered to repair the back end of the red garage, but he did chop down the peach tree.

The first time, I tried to drive the tractor, I commandeered it alone, because I knew I could drive it and I wanted to surprise everyone with my expertise. And the tractor had been left (in reverse gear) sitting out in the peach orchard.

Then it actually started. The tractor flew across the field backwards. It was a startling ride, but hitting a tree and hearing the trunk crack unraveled my theory of driving expertise.

The tractor choked to a stop. I got off, went inside, passed mother at her sewing machine, mumbled that I felt like I was getting sick, went to my room and got ready for bed. It was four o'clock. Nobody ever woke me up to spank me.

Mother stopped sewing and went to see what I had done. When she came back inside, she came to the door of my room and said that staying in my room was a good idea. I covered my head with the sheet and lay there. My fate was sealed.

One of my problems learning to drive the tractor was that the speed was controlled by a little handle that controlled the gas. The handle was near the big old steering wheel. You were supposed to pull back the handle and cut the flow of gas when you were about to slow down or stop.

When the tree was forgotten and only a sawed off trunk w as a reminder, I began to beg to drive the tractor. Finally, I cajoled my brother Will to let me drive the tractor from the field one day when he had finished plowing. He unhooked the plow and lifted me into the seat.

Wow! He hollered instructions as we lurched past the barn, chugged through squawking chickens and barking dogs. Animals know when things are askew.

I did have a perfect bead on the red garage. I did not hit any of the support beams or the sides. However, at a critical moment, I did forget to slow down the tractor. I heard Will curse for the first time when the tractor impacted the back wall. I got off the tractor while Will was inspecting for structural damage and went on inside and went to bed.

Judy Rozzelle

The Farm All Tractor, Continued

Like many members of my family, I learned to drive on Pop-Pop's 1941 Farm All tractor. Pop-Pop stopped what he was doing one summer afternoon while I was sitting on the tractor and came over to show me how to get it cranked and going. Then he went about his chores. I could drive it all right. That was easy. It was not long, however, before it dawned on me that I didn't know how to stop it. Pop-Pop hadn't showed me that. Stopping this particular tractor was not as easy as stomping on a brake.

The brake was hand-operated and located to the right of the steering wheel. For what seemed like hours, I rode in circles and screamed for Pop-Pop. Finally, he heard my hollering and came to my aid. But my problems were not over. I had to put the tractor up in the shed. I missed the entrance on the first pass and drove right through the side of the building. I felt real bad until Pop-Pop told me that my Aunt Judy drove the tractor through the back of the shed when she was first learning to drive. And that was after she had knocked down a peach tree. To this day, whenever I get on my own tractor, I think of that summer afternoon and my grandfather.

Frank Rozzelle

Will Runs Over Harry

Yvonne and I were about eight or nine years old when Will ran over Harry. We were playing out by the old garage where dad kept the tractor and three cars. The cars were used to deliver paper routes. It was an old building with a storage place on one end, a place for the tractor and then room for three cars to park. It was painted red with leftover barn paint.

It was in the afternoon. Momma and Aunt Mutt were inside the house cutting out dresses to sew for their girls. Yvonne and I were playing in the basketball court that was in the chicken yard. We were throwing the basketball at the chickens more often than the goal post. Anne was three. She was sitting on the steps of the granary being good. Harry was about two years old, and obviously, we didn't know what he was doing. We were kids, they were kids, we were vaguely aware that they had left the house with us. But after that, we were distracted.

Will was a good-looking, cool older brother. He must have been seventeen. When he came around Yvonne and I just stared and asked if we could hang around. But today he was going somewhere. He spoke to us and jumped in his car.

Harry was two and had crawled under the car to inspect it. Will backed the car out and over Harry, but he did not run over Harry. However, that is not what Yvonne and I saw. Will stopped the car when we screamed. Harry sat up and laughed, but we were off.

We ran to the house with the news so quickly we couldn't catch our breath when we got inside. Our mothers were gathered around the kitchen table with a dress pattern laid on cloth. They were both cutting out pieces of a dress pattern from material spread out on the dinning room table. They straightened up and looked at us. We took a deep breath and screamed in unison, "Will ran over Harry."

Aunt Mutt fainted.

My mother's scream sounded like a five o'clock whistle. Will came inside carrying a giggling Harry.

Yvonne and I sat down on the sofa and got real quiet. We knew. When the chaos and panic subsided, our mothers took us by the upper part of our arms and led us to rooms in different parts of the house…for a talk. It was one of those talks where you are confined for an hour to think it over.

Judy Rozzelle

Judy, The Overprotective Mom

Mom was just plain overprotective when we were growing up. If I was ever dumb enough to tell her when there was trouble between my friends and me, she'd get in the middle of it and try to fix it. I learned to keep my mouth shut by the time I was five years old, if not sooner. But my brother took a lot longer to learn to keep his mouth shut. I remember the day he began to catch on to the wisdom of silence.

Mom had just gotten home from work. She was changing clothes in the bedroom and Jenny was waiting for Mom to drive her home. The table was set for supper and Teeny and I were packing up the Barbie doll clothes. Then Brad burst into the back door hollering, "Tony took my motorcycle away from me."

The motorcycle was a small green Honda QA 50 and we were the envy of the neighborhood because of it. Tony was older by three years and he was the local bully.

Brad should have kept his mouth shut and later shot at Tony with his BB gun or something. I am sure the two of us could have figured out something to do to get even.

Mom heard him hollering and she came running out of the bedroom charging like a bull that had just seen a red flag. Wearing only her slip, she blasted through the kitchen and out the screen door like a rocket.

Teeny and I ran outside along with Jenny and my desperate brother. Can you imagine how awful it would be to see your mom wearing a slip, heading across the backyard to beat up the neighborhood bully?

Jenny caught on to the seriousness of it all immediately. She was hollering at Mom at the top of her voice and waving Mom's dress, "Judy, come back here right now and put on your dress." Mom kept running. "I know you hear me, Judy. Come back here right now."

Brad was just ahead of Jenny and behind Mom. He was hollering, "I'll run away from home if you beat up Tony Huffstetler."

Mom began to slow down, but she was still screaming and marching towards battle, "Tony Huffstetler, bring that motorcycle here to me, right now." Tony was looking at her with his mouth hanging open.

Jenny caught up with Mom in the apple tree grove by the barn. She grabbed the hem of Mom's slip. Mom stopped dead in her tracks. I think she was as afraid of Jenny as Brad and me were. It was just best not to anger Jenny.

Jenny slammed the dress over Mom's head while Brad made his point about running away from home. He talked as fast as a New York cabdriver and, all the while, he was climbing up the apple tree and out onto the lowest limb. When Mom straightened up, Brad was hanging in her face, "Mom, I mean it, if you take that motorcycle away from Tony I will run away tonight while you are asleep."

Mom was muttering under her breath and Jenny was saying, "You know better than to throw a hissy fit in front of your children and with nothing on but your slip. Sometimes I think you don't have good sense."

Jenny then took charge. "Supper is on the table. This family is going to eat right now. Brad, go get your motorcycle. Tony, you go home, you hear me. Now."

Mom walked home a step behind Jenny. Brad got wise that day and began to keep things to himself.

Cousin Yvonne is right about one thing. Sometimes Mom would act like an idiot, but it was a lot of fun to watch.

Roz Sanders

Yvonne And Judy Have Sex

Diane Neighbors told all the kids in the neighborhood about sex. Yvonne and I were usually there when the subject came up. We got the concept.

Two people get naked, get in bed and get on top of each other. Yvonne had a hard time figuring out how the act of stacking two naked bodies made you pregnant with a baby. We decided that Diane did not know all that much about sex in the first place. However, we were still fascinated with the subject. We figured the adults were pulling our legs when they said they found us under a tree in the pasture.

The subject of sex usually came up in the summertime when we had all day to play and time to discuss things. We talked about sex underneath shade trees by the creek pitching rocks or in Diane's front yard where we drew pictures in the dirt with sticks. Sometime around nine o'clock on a Saturday morning.

Yvonne and I never dropped a subject easily. Sometimes we arrived with list of questions for Diane, but mostly her answer was, "I reckon so." This sex thing was a real problem for us. We just couldn't figure out what was such fun about it. We certainly never believed this was something our parents would do. Not even on a dare.

Once a week Yvonne spent the night with me, one particularly hot night when we both were about eight, the subject of sex was on our minds. The night was so hot that the smell of honeysuckle filled the air like a scented candle.

Yvonne said, "Maybe it's because we don't have breasts yet is why we can't get excited about sex." "Maybe. You think we'll have big ones?" I asked. "We will just have to wait and hope," she said.

Mom called us to come down for our baths. An hour later, we were lying in bed in just our cotton pajama bottoms with an electric fan in the window blowing heat across our bodies. I have no idea who came up with the suggestion. I will point no fingers but on this hot summer night, Yvonne and I agreed to get naked and lie on top of each other. We had to see what the big deal was about sex. We rotated and each tried being on top. Boy, it was hot and sticky. We sat up and said, "Yuck," at the same time.

"That was awful," Yvonne said." We agreed that sex was not fun, and no one had to worry about us ever doing it again. We rolled over, put on our pajamas, and swore to never, ever, tell anyone. Cross our heart and put a needle in our eye. We were damn sure from that time

44

forward that sex was not for us. A couple of days later Yvonne asked if we could be pregnant, but we never got a big belly.

We built forts for the rest of the summer and didn't ask any more questions about sex.

Judy Rozzelle

Lightning Made Aunt Kacky Tremble

When Mom and Aunt Mutt wanted to go to town, they would ask Aunt Kacky to baby-sit us. Several times, when she kept us in the summer a late afternoon thunderstorm would roll across the sky. At first, she say, "The angels are moving furniture in heaven." When the thunder rumbled for more than a few seconds, she would say, "Oops, somebody dropped something."

She was trying to comfort herself as much as us. But when the lightning scratched across the sky Aunt Kacky got up from her rocking chair and told us to get underneath the narrow tin-topped kitchen table. I don't think Aunt Kacky ever knew that tin carried lightning or she didn't care.

Often, our moms arrived home to find the three of us sitting under the kitchen table. If we weren't snapping beans, our heads were bowed in prayer while Aunt Kacky pleaded for God to make the storm pass.

Yvonne Rozzelle Herbert

Church Camp

There was only one summer camp for us rural kids, and that was church camp Camp Stewart, it was called. We lived in the remotest corner of a kudzu-choked forest north of Shuffletown for a week of Bible study, evening vespers, and, on Saturday evening, skits. Presbyterians ran it. Our parents gave us no choice.

The actual camp wasn't much. You could call it rustic, but it was downright primitive. We slept in tin-roofed cabins built on fieldstone foundations. There were paths, well worn, leading from each cabin to a cement-floored community bathroom. It had nowhere near enough individual shower stalls. And never, not once in that long, long week, did all the commodes flush properly. One or two was always plugged. I do not remember what I learned of Jesus Our Lord and Savior's life back then, but I will never forget how the bathroom smelled.

I attended Camp Stewart with my cousin Yvonne. Yvonne from an early age was one of those children adults believed to be without malice. I knew better. But I will say she wasn't afraid of Evil and we were exposed to a lot of it at church camp. Every night our counselors would fill our heads not with images of the Christ child or stories of his apostles but instead, all manner of ghost stories involving chicken-headed ladies, bloodthirsty vampires, or pirates wandering around with swords through their eye sockets. I would listen to tales that made me want to cry, made me want to go home, made me stay awake for all 168 hours spent at camp while Yvonne yawned, totally unfazed. When the story was finished, our counselor would have us all get down on our knees and recite the Lord's Prayer. I don't think anybody, with the exception of men in foxholes, has ever recited the Lord's Prayer with such fervor and hope as we seven cabin mates leaving out Yvonne, of course, who was asleep before the amen.

Yvonne was in perfect control of not only her mind but also mine, on occasion. There was a nice boy who rode our school bus, Dale Gordon, who was older, fourteen at least. He had a crush on me. I didn't really fancy him I was in love with Tommy White, forever, cross my heart and hope to die but Yvonne got it into her head that Dale was the perfect mate for me. She decided that, during this week at Camp Stewart, I should declare my love for him and reserve him for a wedding sometime in the next decade.

One morning as we sat rocking in chairs outside the camp store, writing postcards home—I was furiously scribbling Come get me, please?—Yvonne announced her plan.

"Judy?" She said, pursing her lips in that my-mind's-made-up way of hers. "You ought to send Dale a card. Tell him how much you care for him and tell him you think there is a great future for you two."

"Who?" I was underlining the phrase, Come get me NOW.

"Dale Gordon. His daddy is a preacher and that would be good."

I do not recall what she said to convince me this was a good idea. She must have told me it would get me home sooner, because fifteen minutes later, I had declared my undying love to this boy on the back of a two-cent postcard and mailed it.

Just as it slid out of my hand and down the chute, I experienced, for the first time in my life, second thoughts, the sensation of sinking regret. In the next couple decades, I married many men, but Dale, you can be sure, was not one of them.

But I got even with Cousin.

Every afternoon that week of camp, we had about an hour of free time before supper. Yvonne and I always headed to an oversized swing hung by ropes from the limb of a massive tree. The seat was so large we could stand facing each other, grab each rope, and pump. Boy, could we make that sucker swing. There were times, I swear, when it seemed like it was almost horizontal with the ground. The wind rushed past us and we held on for dear life. But we were young and invincible, so we kept pushing it a little higher, and a little faster, each day.

Well, one afternoon, just as we were swinging past Mars, the limb cracked. Yvonne always recalled that I landed on top of her. She hurt her neck. I hurt my back. People came running. The adults stood us up, brushed off our clothes, and asked us if we were trying to kill ourselves. They checked us for broken bones and then formed a circle around the swing to debate whether or not to fix it. Yvonne and I staggered off to supper.

Three decades later, a doctor convinced my cousin to have the cracked vertebrae in her neck repaired. After the operation, I went to see her. She was heavily sedated, but she rose from her pillow and pointed her finger at me like the ghost of Banquo.

"You did this to me when the swing broke! You landed on my frigging head, you idiot. This is all your fault."

"Yeah, well!" I sputtered. "YOU shouldn't have made me mail that postcard!" I rubbed my back, which still hurts me whenever it rains or I get worked up.

"Oh, yeah," she said, dropping back on her pillow and closing her eyes. "I forgot that postcard." A smile spread over her face. Then she drifted off into a drugged sleep.

Judy Rozzelle

Home Remedies

When we got the chills, Mother would find a pine tree that had been cut and bleeding sap. She would roll the pine resin into little balls and give it to whoever was sick. It worked. Try it some time, but you try any of the kerosene medicine mother used, you had better have pure kerosene, not the stuff they sell today.

Daisy Aaron Black

J.E.R.K.

It was not the first time Yvonne got the best of me. It was the first time she drew blood. I scored a couple of hits in our life-long game of wit, but I recall clearly the first time Yvonne defined the game for me.

It was a clear, blue-sky day. I know where I was standing and I can still feel the air seeping out of me like a pierced balloon. In that moment, I knew life with Cousin Yvonne would be a bumpy ride and alertness was required.

We were nine years old, it was the end of summer and we were about to enter the third grade at Long Creek Elementary School. Mom had taken me shopping for new school shoes and school supplies. I had missed the whole afternoon of playing with the kids. But it was always exciting purchasing new school supplies, plaid book satchels, binders, pencils and pens for cursive writing. It was the only day I ever thought school was a good idea.

After we had purchased a new pair of shoes, I begged Mother to let me spend my month's allowance on a pink suede belt with my initials. Then, I watched excitedly as the sales clerk glued my initials, JER, onto the belt in big black letters. I could not wait to get home and show it off.

It was late in the day and, I knew, the kids would be gathered beneath the big oak tree at Ruby's home on the dead end road. It was the time of day when play was mostly done. Too late to begin a new adventure and too soon to go home. It was time to sit and wait to hear your Mother call you to come home for chores. It was when laundry was removed from the clothesline, chickens were fed, potatoes were peeled, and the table was set.

The moment Mom brought the car to a stop in our driveway, I opened the door and jumped out. I could hear Mom calling for me to come right back and help her start supper, but I was running down the narrow footpath past the chicken house scattering chickens, past the barn, through the cornfield and the field of cantaloupes to the dead end road. I was going to show off my new belt. Before they came into sight I was hollering, "Hey, y'all." There they were under the oak tree in Ruby's front yard. The tree's old roots threaded in and out of the yard and anchored our world of friendship, adventure and fantasy.

Ruby had begun her chores. She was behind the house taking sheets off the clothes line, but she turned and waved. Yvonne and Judi were tracing circles in the dirt with sticks under the oak tree. The boys were shooting marbles next to them. I crossed the road, jumped the ditch, ran towards the tree, put my hands on my hips, stuck out my stomach and asked, "Whatyadoing?"

Yvonne looked up. "Did you get your school stuff?"

"Yeah," I answered, "but look at this cool belt I got with my initials on it."

Everyone looked. Yvonne gazed in my direction, studied my wonderful new belt, and said, "Judy, if you marry someone with a last name that starts with a 'K', your initials will spell JERK."

I could only hear the sound of escaping air.

Judy Rozzelle

Growing Up Country

I believe growing up in the country was a blessing. Each night I'd lie upstairs in my bed on my old feather mattress and fight sleep, waiting for the quiet to set in for the night. Quiet. That dark silence, when you can hear a leaf fall from a tree, doesn't happen in an instant. You have to wait for it.

It takes patience to wait on quiet. You have to stay awake long enough for the dogs to settle down, for the cats to stop caterwauling and curl up on the back porch steps to doze. Around 1 a.m., the night creatures the crickets, the cicadas would stop calling to each other.

You could hear the milk train over about Mt. Holly. Its lonely whistle would pierce the darkness. As the dark settled on the land and I began to sink into the down of the pillows and mattress, quiet would hush the land. And down by Long Creek the daddy bullfrogs would call to each other.

One bullfrog would call to the other across the pond, "Come over, come over." Another bullfrog, lazy as the first, would call back, "Go 'round, go 'round." You see, neither one of them wanted to move. My granddaddy taught me that. They could holler all night but they never got together. Bullfrogs are stubborn creatures.

By then it was quiet and dark; my world had gone to sleep. In early fall I could hear the leaves break from the tree outside my window. The window curtains billowed with a gust of wind. It was quiet enough to hear yourself think, and silent enough to remember your thoughts.

Zeke Cooper

Cousins

Cousin Yvonne and I were born in Shuffletown in 1941. Cousins were as common as robins back then, but almost from birth, the two of us were locked in a world of sibling rivalry once removed.

Our lifelong quest was to prove to the world that "this other cousin" had been born missing a couple of vital genes. Some say she won, there might not have been a clear winner, but there was always an audience.

Our other cousins just enjoyed the show Yvonne and I produced in our lifelong competition. It just ended too soon. We were too soon grown and she was too soon gone.

Judy Rozzelle

Mama Jo and
her girls

Pop Pop's
home

Christmas of
long ago

We never lose a foundation!
Volunteer Fire Department

Groundbreaking for a new church

The Big House, Rozzelles Ferry Inn

Bones and his
private tub

Eating daisies
as a snack

Rob's first pet

My aunts, a dog, and a visitor

Aunt Kacky and Grandma
on the ferry,
going to church

Church in the vale

Bringing in the sheaves

Home Sweet Home

Replica of Rozzelles Ferry

First
Pony

Rob and
the calf

Pop Pop
and Judy

Grandpa Rozzelle

Elizabeth Rozzelle

The Grant Sisters:
Henrietta, GG,
and Jenny

Blonnie Rozzelle
(photo by
Bobbie Stillwell)

Pop-Pop's barn

His school photo

His swing

Another day at Shuffletown Grocery
(photo by Ron Rozzelle)

Shuffletown Grocery

Housework
began at
sunrise

The pond

Merry Christmas

Grandmother Aaron

Mama Aaron

Reverend Aaron

The barn
was torn
down first

Home in the country

Shuffletown crossroads - 1940

Rozzelles Ferry Bridge

The first fire truck was purchased from Pinoca

Announcing Shuffletown's Mayday Mayday Festival
and Yard Sale

photo by Ron Rozzelle

The Cameron Family

Cameron Circle

The Cameron family once owned most of the land just past the bridge at Shuffletown Drag Strip. That is, they owned what the Fullers and the Spencers did not own. They named their area Cameron Circle and set about populating it. Now, there are too many Camerons to count, and it is well known that they all love to play tricks on each other. However, you could say Slick and Jim Bob Cameron raised the bar when it came to practical jokes.

You see, Slick was the youngest of Scott Cameron's ten children. When Slick's older brother Scott Jr. left to fight in WWII, he deposited his wife and son, Jim Bob, into the elder Scott Cameron's home. Jim Bob was only a year younger than Slick and Slick thought Jim Bob was another brother. A smaller brother he could pick on, kind of like a toy. For the next two years, the two boys slept together, played together and generally aggravated each other from dawn to dusk as brothers will do.

When the war was over, Scott retrieved his wife and Jim Bob, and took them back to their home across the street. Slick would not sleep alone that first night, so he went home with Scott also. In the next couple of months, they slept at one home or the other and continued to act more like brothers than an uncle and a nephew. Eventually, Slick did get used to sleeping alone in his home. But growing up, or at least aging, never dampened their enthusiasm for playing picking on each other.

Abby Rozzelle

This Is How It All Started

When Scott came home from the war and Jim Bob went home, I really was upset. He lived just across the road, but that did not matter. Now, I had to go across the road to pick on him. I was the youngest of the ten Cameron children, which makes me Jim Bob's uncle, but heck I was only a year older than him. My brother Scott was the oldest Cameron, and he was twenty years older than me. Anyway, Jim Bob and I kept acting like brothers.

When we got old enough, Jim Bob and me loved to go into the woods and find the Christmas trees. Jim Bob and I always competed to see who got the biggest tree. I usually found the biggest tree, but sometimes he did.

One Christmas, I was the first to spot and tag a great tree, the best ever. Chick Poole was with us. We were still young and acting like kids. Somebody was installing a pipeline and Chick and I were walking across the pipe balancing the tree on our shoulders. We had our rifles with us to shoot down some mistletoe. Jim Bob was dragging his tree and had his rifle on his shoulder. Somehow, and I swear this happened, his gun fired and he shot the top out of my tree. He could not do that if he had tried. I gave him my tree and took his. To use the tree, he had to wire the top back into it, and it turned out to be one ugly tree.

Jim Bob and Betty decorated it and it stood in front of his picture window. I called everybody I knew to have them call Jim Bob collect to tell him they drove by his house and they wanted him to know that that was the ugliest Christmas tree they had ever seen. The two of us had an oil business back then and we were used to accepting collect phone calls.

I had truckers call him collect from Texas, Tennessee and Michigan to tell him that was the ugliest Christmas tree they had ever seen. I even had my in-laws call him collect from New York to tell him what an ugly Christmas tree he had. Everyone called collect at all times night and day. It drove him nuts not to mention the phone bill for December.

Jim Bob hated to chop wood. So, every fall, he would load his kids in his pickup truck and go around to everybody's house. He and the kids would jump out and take as much wood as they could in a few minutes. All you ever saw was Jim Bob's truck tearing down your driveway with his kids laughing in the back. He went to Chick's house, Skeet's house, Don Fuller's house and mine. The last person he stopped at always called to tell me they were on the way. One time I hid behind the wood pile and when they finished loading the wood, I jumped up with my gun and hollered. I really felt bad about how much I scared his kids. So I laid low for a while.

Jim Bob and I once added Ex-Lax to a chocolate cake and took it to a Shriners Convention. Don Fuller was also a Shriner and he was prone to steal food from our room. We knew he would steal the cake. He did as expected and shared it with everyone who came by his hotel room.

He gave half of it to some big Potentate who was supposed to ride a camel in the parade. But when it was time for the parade, they were all trotting back and forth to bathrooms. The Potentate did not ride the camel because he was in the bathroom when the parade left. We never told anyone what was in the cake because we knew they would kill us or worse, get even.

Well, I remembered the cake and whipped up a pan of Ex-Lax brownies. Ever tried it? It does add flavor and consistency. I wrapped up three brownies and left them on the floor of my truck. They were half hidden under a brick.

Well, Jim Bob was delivering oil that day and he said that by noon he was crapping under every other house. Sometimes he said he would be under the house and the customer would start talking to him from the kitchen window. He said he could pump oil, crap and carry on a conversation at the same time. I knew he would retaliate, but nothing happened for a long time and I dropped my guard.

Slick Cameron

Quick Trot Brownies

If you asked me to remember all the pranks Slick and I have pulled on each other, well, that would be impossible. We started young. You see Mom and me lived with Grandma and Grandpa Cameron when Dad was in the war. Slick and me were so young we thought we were brothers. And we picked on each other like brothers do.

We've been daring each other and tricking each other since we could walk, probably started when we were crawling. Some pranks, I just can't tell you about. But I can tell you about what all began when Slick's wife decided Slick had to lose some weight.

Then she got on this idea to feed him stuff that was good for him. When Slick was ready to bust out the door in the morning, she would hand him an apple instead of a biscuit. He never ate it. He would throw it on the dashboard and stop for a sausage and egg biscuit on the way to work. He ate out a lot in those days.

During the day, I would go in his truck, eat the apple and leave the core. Well, sometimes I got a little more inventive. Couple of times, I dug up some earthworms, slit the apple open, drop it on the floorboard and dump the earthworms on top of it. No matter what I did, Slick never said anything about it. That is part of the game, you know.

One morning, I was on my way to deliver oil. I got in his truck to get my apple and, by God, there were brownies wrapped in tin foil. Mighty good brownies too, they even had nuts in them. They were

53

partially hidden under a brick. I ate 'em all and left a mess of crumbs in his truck.

I was crawling under Mr. Spurrier's house when they kicked in. My stomach suddenly began to ache and cramp like a foundered horse. That jackass, Slick, had put a laxative in the brownies and a lot of it. I was afraid I was going to blow myself out from under the house.

At first, I stopped in service stations to use the bathroom, but I was under duress. And man, I was having a hard time. What I am telling you is that I did have to crap under some good people's houses. I tell you no lie, a couple of times, I would be under a house filling the oil tank, crapping and someone would holler, "Hello, Jim Bob, how you doing?" from their kitchen window. So, I had to add talking to my chores while I finished my business. I did flag the houses where I answered the call to nature so I could come back later and throw some sand on it.

When I got back to the office, Slick called from his office, "Jim Bob, how was your day?"

"Just fine," I answered. "I got the oil delivered." But I was thinking about revenge.

Jim Bob Cameron

Turkey Trot

That Jim Bob, I could have killed him. It was a cold November morning and I was running late. Good Lord, you would not believe what I saw when I opened the door to my truck.

Jim Bob had struck during the night. He stuck a wild turkey inside my truck and locked it inside. He had tied the brick from the brownies to a rope and tied it to the turkey's neck.

That turkey crapped all over my truck. It smelled horrible. I yanked the turkey out of my truck, backed it out of the garage, hosed it out, seats, windows, every inch of it. When I could sit inside it without gagging, I drove off in it.

When I got to the office, Jim Bob had coffee and doughnuts waiting. I sat down, ate three doughnuts, drank my coffee and asked, "Did the Hornets beat Jacksonville last night?"

"Naw," he answered. "They can't beat anybody."

However, on the home front, I had forgot about the turkey and left it in the garage. When my wife came out to do the laundry, the turkey had had about all he could take. She said he would fly at her and then poop. The turkey just kept gobbling and pooping. Hell, she panicked and dialed 911, plus she called Critter Control. I cleaned up feathers and crap for two weeks. I had to teach that boy a lesson, once and for all, and Christmas was just around the corner.

Slick Cameron

It Was Christmas Eve

I knew he was up to something, but it was Christmas Eve and I did not want to alarm the family. Slick was late arriving. He was about an hour and a half late and I knew he had done something. I just did not know what.

Jim Bob Cameron

Reindeer On The Roof

After the turkey business, I devised a prank that deserved an award. Jim Bob and I were now selling big equipment to contractors and such. I asked around and found an old Santa type-sleigh and I bought two mangy goats. The goats weren't hard to come by. A couple of guys helped me, Wit Wiley and Dean. Christmas Eve, after Jim Bob had left his house to go to the Cameron gathering. I called my sister, Mae, and said I was going to be late. I think she knew I was up to something, 'cause she said, "Whatever you're up to better not harm anything or cost money."

Wit loaded up the sleigh in his truck and went for the goats. I worked the forklift and Dean operated the cherry picker. It took an hour, but we finally got the antlers wired on the goats' heads. I called them Prancer and Dancer and they didn't look too bad. You would think they were reindeer, if you were standing out by the road. Wit scattered feed and hay on the roof. Pretty soon, we had the whole outfit on Jim Bob's roof. It was a real Christmas scene.

I almost forgot the brick, but just in time, I remember to tie the brick to a rope and hung it off his roof with a Christmas card. I didn't sign it. I got to the old home place in time for supper. Jim Bob acted calm, but I knew he was worried.

Slick Cameron

Prancer And Dancer

We got home close to midnight. There were cars lining both sides of the road, and there was a TV news team in my front yard filming my roof for the late news.

"Dad, are those reindeer?" my youngest piped up from the back seat. We just sat in the car in the driveway watching. There were goats and a sled on my rooftop. The goats seemed to be grazing quite happily. It was a contented scene, except the antlers that had been tied around each goat's head had slipped sideways.

It was snowing and the whole crazy sight was almost pretty. But I knew that I would have to get it all down tomorrow unless Santa Claus did it when he stopped by.

Eventually, the camera crews and the spectators left. But we had a rough night. The sound of hooves clomping around on the roof kept waking us up, and I lay there praying the whole thing did not fall in on top of us before morning.

Around seven a.m., an ice storm moved in. It sleeted and froze most of Christmas Day. Around noon, the goats began eating my shingles. They ate pretty near all the shingles on the carport. By New Year's, most folks in these parts and a few from out of town had driven by the house. While my wife took down the Christmas tree, I took down the goats. I got it all down including a lot of goat manure and the brick with the Christmas card tied to it. Christmas Day, Slick had wisely chosen to go out of town for a week of skiing. But he could not hide from me, and he knew it.

Jim Bob Cameron

I'd Rather Eat Crow

Betty, Jim Bob's wife, called a week before Jim Bob's birthday to ask me to help her give him a surprise birthday party. I agreed to keep Jim Bob busy all day that Saturday and bring him up to the river cabin around six for a surprise birthday party.

I drove that boy all over Mecklenburg County visiting people. I was tired when we pulled into the river place. Everybody was already there and I thought we'd pulled off the surprise pretty good. At least, Jim Bob acted surprised.

We all had a beer while Jim Bob cooked the burgers. He asked each of us how we liked ours cooked. Betty and the women had us all sit down while they brought out the food and they even put all the fixings on our hamburgers.

I was tired and hungry. I picked up that bun and took a big bite out of the hamburger. It was the worst thing I ever tasted. It tasted too awful to swallow and there was grit in the meat. I couldn't swallow it and it kept getting bigger in my mouth. I looked around and from the look on everybody's face, they felt the same way. Lord, what a taste.

Then Jim Bob ran around the table taking pictures of everyone. He took mine first and then I knew I had been had. His birthday is in April. Christmas was long past and I didn't suspect a thing.

Betty set a breadbasket down in front of me with the brick in it. All of us bolted out the door and puked. We were cussing like mule trainers and Jim Bob was standing on the porch laughing and taking pictures.

"What do you think that was?" Wit asked.

"I don't know," I answered. "And I don't want to know."

Jim Bob threw us each a beer to wash our mouths out. When we got back inside I looked in the breadbasket; there was the damn brick. Then I looked at the hamburger and it was the ugliest thing I had ever seen. Not only was it filled with bone and grizzle, there was hair sticking out of it.

Jim Bob had taken one of the goats to Sheriff Dan's abattoir and had it ground into hamburger. Not just the meat, he had the whole goat ground up, hair, tail, skull, everything. It also looked like he might have drug it through the yard. It was nasty. It makes me want to puke just to think of it. I should've thrown the brick at him, but he was too happy. It was his birthday and he did finally serve us steaks.

Slick Cameron

Sweet Revenge

That was sweet revenge, but I had to stay on my toes. There was no telling what Slick would do next. I just it would be good and I hoped it didn't cost me too much.

Jim Bob Cameron

A Prank To End All Pranks

I knew a man in Greensboro who owned an elephant. Not two days after the goat burger, I had him on the phone and rented the elephant for July 4th. I was going to put it in Jim Bob's back yard or his garage, if it would fit. Then I sat back and waited for time to pass. About June, the man called and his elephant had died.

I was calling around trying to find another elephant when the wives and Jim Bob walked into the office. Jim Bob was rolling his eyes and the women looked dead set on something. You've seen wives with that look; it means you are going to clean out the garage or paint the porch. Today.

Jim Bob turned a chair around and sat down. The girls sat on the couch.

"What's up?" I asked. "Jim Bob looks like he is a prisoner."

"He is," Betty answered.

Then my wife opened her mouth. "Slick, this brick joke stuff has gone far enough."

"Not yet, it hasn't," I answered.

My wife then told Jim Bob about the dead elephant.

"Would have been a good joke. Where would you have put it?" Jim Bob asked.

"I was figuring on the back yard or your garage," I answered. "I'm trying to find another one."

"Oh no, you are not," the women screamed in unison.

Then they moaned about this and that and what could happen. Women stuff. An hour later, I dug a hole in the yard in front of the office. Jim Bob said a few words about the exciting life of the brick, but before he finished our wives took the shovel, threw the dirt back in the hole. Both of them jumped up and down on the grave then pranced off together to go shopping.

We thought about digging it up but thought better of it. Anyhow, we knew it would take more than burying a brick to stop us. We decided to go to lunch and check into a headstone for the brick.

Slick Cameron

Surely, Our Wives Were Joking

Slick and I did not intend to stop our pranks. We were just going to lay low for a while.

Jim Bob Cameron

Tragedy Strikes And The Brick is Buried

I couldn't believe it when the call came in on the office phone. Jim Bob had had a heart attack in the Chicago airport and died on the spot, before they could even get help. He had been returning from a sales call. His father, Scott, had also died suddenly of a heart attack, but we never dreamed it would happen to him, also. He was too young. He was forty-eight years old.

For a long time, I just sat by the phone, stunned. Finally, I went on home and we all drove over to the old home place to be with the family. I just can't tell you how it felt. I don't think I even believed it until Jim Bob arrived at the funeral home the next day.

The night before the funeral, the family received friends at the funeral home. I couldn't do anything but shake people's hands and nod in response. That night, after everyone had gone home, I went and dug up the brick.

It was late when I got back to the funeral home, alone. They let me sit with Jim Bob. I held our brick and talked to him for the longest time about all the good times we had. I even apologized for the reindeer stunt. I sat there until I knew what I wanted to do with the brick was right. Jim Bob would have done the same for me. I would have expected it.

I miss that boy. I guess I always will.

Slick Cameron

Uncles

It was great growing up with all my crazy Cameron uncles. You never knew what crazy stunt they were going to pull on each other or me. Well, it was great until I followed them into high school. The teachers remembered all of them, especially the teachers who were older than dirt and had taught school forever. At the beginning of each class, when they called the roll and got to my name, they'd ask, "Are you related to the Cameron boys?"

Well, I'm proud of my family so that first year in high school, I answered with a firm, "Why yes, I am." That one answer caused me all kinds of trouble. Every one of those teachers watched me like a hawk for the rest of the year. I couldn't get away with even a yawn without being punished.

Mrs. Roddy was so old, she couldn't hear anything, but she remembered everything about the Cameron boys. If a plane flew overhead, she didn't even hear it. She couldn't hear a thunderstorm outside, but let me open my mouth to whisper and she'd say, "Jack Cameron, shut up and come up here."

At the beginning of my sophomore year when someone asked if I was related to the Cameron boys I'd answer, "No, I just moved here from Georgia."

Jack Cameron

Cameron Christmas Eve Tradition

The tradition began in 1951. The family had outgrown the bed of a pickup truck for the Christmas season's festivities. Mr. Cameron hooked a trailer to his tractor, filled it with hay and drove the many members of the Cameron family to Christmas Eve services at Sloan Memorial Presbyterian Church. For a decade, they came to Christmas Eve Services in the trailer, and on the way home stopped by their neighbors and sang carols.

By 1962, they had outgrown the trailer and Uncle Scott Cameron decided they needed a big truck. He procured a flat bed truck. They threw in the hay, hung on to the little ones and merrily rode to the Christmas Eve Services.

When the number of Camerons was more than fifty, they borrowed Eli Wallen's biggest truck, filled it with hay, grandchildren, nephews and nieces, and sang to each other all the way to church.

In 1964, Uncle David Cameron managed to obtain a larger truck and at least sixty Camerons piled into the back of the truck to go to Christmas Eve services. They don't know how, but Uncle David Cameron got lost on the way home and they spent an hour riding around in the open bed of a dump truck while singing loud enough to shake snow from tree limbs and startle sleeping birds.

By the 70s, the Camerons were renting a U-Haul trailer to get to church on Christmas Eve. Their arrival was a strange sight. Slick or David was usually driving. Jarrell and Jim Bob were often also seen in the front seat. During the mile long ride to church, I am sure each had a chance to drive.

When they arrived at the church, the drivers would jump out of the front seat and run around, raise the big back door to the trailer and Camerons piled out of the hay like clowns out of a clown car. It was not Christmas Eve at church until the Camerons arrived, brushed hay from their clothes, and entered the church. Then, and only then did the Christmas Eve service begin.

Judy Rozzelle

The Art of Marriage

Helpmates

Country people called their spouses "helpmates." The term also appears in the King James Version of the *Holy Bible*. It sounds simple, but its practical implications are enormous.

Couples who are compatible and working towards a common goal help each other. Extra hands are needed to help raise crops, to help tend animals, to help bring up children and to help lay things by for the winter. Survival depends on being able to divide the tasks without rancor or problems of dominance. This system depends on good will and love between the spouses.

Gail E. Haley

Bud And Libby Clockman

Back when we were young and it began to get cold, we'd watch for Bob and Libby Clockman to build their first fire. When we saw the gray smoke trailing out of their chimney, we knew the time had arrived to sit with them in front of the fire.

We never grew tired of talking to them, or waiting for them to spit. You see, Bob and Libby sat in old rocking chairs directly across from each other in front of the fireplace.

Bob was always whittling on a piece of wood, and Libby was always mending something. Bob chewed tobacco and Libby dipped snuff. She kept a well-chewed gum tree stick to dip snuff with. She called it her toothbrush. She'd take that stick, dip it in her snuff, and stick the snuff in her mouth with it.

Bob just stuck his hand in the tobacco bag, pulled out a plug and stuck it in his mouth. Then we'd sit there watching the fire and talking about things. After a few minutes, Libby would lift her right hand and place her index and middle fingers on her lips.

I guess this helped her aim. Then she would spit into the fireplace. Bob didn't turn his head to look at her. But instinctively he'd lift his head at the same moment as Libby. Their aim was perfect. Their two streams of tobacco juice hit the fire at exactly the same time. We took turns sitting with them by the fire for several winters, and no one ever saw them spit individually. I guess that what comes from being married forever.

Ivy Aaron Barnes

The Clockmans' Passing

She had a stroke, she didn't linger but a couple of days and then she was gone. I was down there when she began to talk to her dead relatives who came to take her home. Mother always called that stage of dying 'calling down the dead." Nowadays we dope the dying all up and they don't get a chance to say goodbye to their family or hello to their angels.

Bob didn't live by himself for long. His nephew, Jake Bain, and his wife, Mary, and their children came to live with him. We knew from the get go that Jake Bain was trifling and no good. He didn't work, but he would disappear for days and he always returned roaring drunk. Momma said he had a whiskey still somewhere in the woods.

When he was drunk, he beat Mary, but there was nothing we could do. In the summertime, our family would sit out on the porch until well past dark.

When Jake Bain came home drunk, we knew there would be trouble. We would hear the little girl, Ruby, crying when it all began. Before long, Mary would be hollering, "Please don't hit me again." Then old Bob would come out on the front porch and just sit with his head in his hands.

Father would rush us off the porch and into the back of the house. Many a night, Father walked down to the log cab in to see if he could stop the beatings. Sometimes, he could, sometimes, he couldn't. Sometimes, he brought Bob home to spend the night with us.

I don't know how Bob put up with it. He was too old and too sad to do anything but stare at the fireplace and spit tobacco on cold ashes. I guess that is what finally killed him. He didn't live four months after Libby died. I am sure dying was a relief for Bob.

Daisy Aaron Black

Rev. Sloan Baptizes His Wife

I was the circuit preacher around these parts. I preached at Shuffletown and Paw Creek. Often I was summoned by a family to their house to marry folks and to baptize new babies. My favorite place,

62

weather permitting, to baptize a baby and to marry a young couple was on the family's front porch. People enjoyed their front porches back then. I baptized Emily Anne Gillis on her Poppa's front porch. It was a beautiful warm day and a vase was nearby was filled with daffodils. She was the prettiest baby I had ever seen. Her momma had her wrapped in white blankets and a lace bonnet held her blonde curls in place.

When I took her from her Poppa she smiled like she was seeing an angel. I swear, she kept smiling at me and she wrapped her tiny hand around my little finger. When I removed the lace cap and sprinkled a little bit of Presbyterian water on her curls, she didn't cry, she laughed joyfully. I felt renewed and I was in love with the woman she would become.

I gave her back to her momma and said, "Take good care of her. I will wait for her and when she is old enough, I will ask her to marry me."

I got on my horse and rode on to the next family in need. It was the prettiest spring day I ever saw. The Good Lord was waking up the good earth. The trees were alive with new yellow-green leaves. It was a grand day to ride your horse down country road spreading the gospel and to meet your future wife. The Lord had predestined our marriage. I had only to wait. And I did wait. We were married when she was twenty-two and I was forty-four. We lived happily ever after. Far as I know, we both fell in love at first sight.

Rev. Sloan Winston

The Bain Family

Our father, Francis Aaron, was the local blacksmith and a lay minister at Nazareth Baptist Church over at Moore's Chapel. And most Sundays he brought someone home to eat with us. Mother was already feeding fifteen kids so I guess a couple more folks didn't matter. After dinner we'd go outside to play and our folks would come sit on the porch to watch the day go by.

We didn't notice one Sunday that Mary had sneaked into our house and locked herself in a bedroom until Jake Bain came out of Bob Clockman's house drunk as a skunk. He walked up the road to our house demanding that we give him his wife. It must have embarrassed Father us having guests and all. He stood up and assured Jake we did not have his wife anywhere on our property. But Jake kept insisting that he had seen her go in by the back door.

63

Finally, Mother and I went inside to look for Mary. We did it just to pacify Jake. But sure enough, the girls' bedroom door was locked from the inside. Finally, after calling to her several times, Mary answered. Mother told her Jake was outside causing a scene and she needed to come out and talk to him.

"I ain't gonna do it," Mary said, and kept the door locked. Mother went outside and spoke to Father. Then he came inside and told Mary she had to leave immediately. After a long silence, I heard her lift the latch, but before we could catch her she shot out the back door and ran into the woods.

Jake Bain saw her and he chased her. She screamed horribly when he caught her. You could hear him hit her from where we were sitting in the front yard. When they came out of the woods he had hold of her hair. She was stumbling and he was mostly dragging her. She was hollering and crying something awful.

Right then, in front of our guests and us kids, when they got to the road, he made her stand up straight and he began to tell her where to put each foot every time she took a step.

He'd say, "Put your right foot here and your left foot there." One time he made her crawl. When that happened Father stood up and hollered, "Jake, stop that right now." But it went on all the way home. He must have beat her when they got inside because we could hear the children crying and Mary hollering. Father suggested that we pray for Mary, and we did pray. Somewhere around sunset, we saw Jake run into the woods and it got quiet in the cabin.

Jake Bain was just trifling and no good. I heard the men say he was a good man when he was sober, but all the kids, not just Jake's kids, were scared of him. He was a mean drunk and a bad man.

But, you know the next day, Monday, when we were all walking home from school. Jake and Mary were laying up under the stand of pine trees in their yard carrying on like sweethearts.

Ivy Aaron Barnes

Mary Bain's Miscarriage

It was early morning when Jake Bain knocked on our back door. Mother and I were fixing breakfast. The coffee was bubbling on the stove and I was rolling out biscuit dough.

Daddy went to the door. I could hear them talking, but I couldn't understand a word. They were talking low but you could tell something was wrong. It wasn't long before Dad came into the kitchen and said,

"Momma, Mary done had a miscarriage. You and Agnes go down to the house and take care of her. Jake and I are going to go get the doctor." My sisters took over the breakfast and we walked down to see Mary.

The ole hound dog was under the back porch and we found Mary in bed. It was a late spring morning, but there was still a chill in the air and we had on coats. Mary had only a tattered sheet covering her. She was shaking like a rattle and sobbing. He had beaten her again. I thought she was dying.

Momma sent me to fetch some water and heat it on the stove. Meanwhile, she began to talk to Mary. She took off her coat and put it around Mary.

Lord, that woman was a mess. She had blood in her hair and blood all over herself. Both of her eyes were swollen and the eyeballs were filled with red blood.

Right there, right beside her under the tattered sheet was a dead baby. It was a young fetus and couldn't have lived, I guess, but it had hair on its head. It was still all curled up and even had its thumb in its mouth.

Momma told me to find a box and the only box I could find was a shoebox filled with string bobbins. I put the stuff in an old pot and took it to Momma. I watched as she laid that tiny little baby inside the box and put it carefully on the cold stove. I still think about that baby who grew inside a human punching bag and died before he was complete.

When the water warmed up, Momma and I washed Mary all over, keeping her covered with the coat while we washed. Pretty soon, Daddy and Jake came in with Dr. Abernethy. While the doctor was talking care of Mary, I stood outside on the back porch. Daddy came outside and he was holding the box with the baby in it. I heard Daddy say, "Jake, we are going to give this baby a Christian burial with prayers asking for God's forgiveness. Let's walk over there to the graveyard find Mary's parents' graves and bury him by them."

"We ain't gonna bury that baby until I look at it and see if it was mine," Jake answered. He grabbed the shoebox and walked out into the sun so he could see well. Daddy and I watched. He took the baby out of the box and stared at it until he was satisfied. Then he put it back in the box, put the lid on it and started walking towards the cemetery.

Momma and I stayed with Mary until we saw everyone walking home from school. I heard Daddy tell Momma at supper that night that Jake was going to kill Mary one of these days.

Daisy Aaron Black

Murder On The Dead End Road

It happened on a Sunday. It had been quiet down at their house recently. Dad said that Jake was out of town on a job. But Daisy saw Jake walking down the road Friday night about sunset. She said he was carrying a jug in each hand and drinking out of both of them. When he got to the front of the house, he fell backward when he tried to step up on the porch. He got up cussing and kicked open the front door.

We didn't see the kids or Mary after that, but we knew things weren't good down there. I heard a couple of my brothers laughing about seeing Jake come out and pee off the porch several times Saturday.

No one saw Mary all weekend. Saturday night there were nice evening breezes. Our whole family sat on the porch long time after dark enjoying the cooler air.

I remember noticing a kerosene lamp flickering inside that troubled dark house. After we had gone to bed, I thought I heard crying from down that way. Sounds can carry a long ways on summer nights.

On Sunday, my family is focused on church and no one thought about the goings on at the Bain house until it happened. Just after dinner, one of the boys came running up the road, hollering that their Daddy had killed their Momma. We all ran down the road towards him. Dad and Momma came out on the porch, calling for us to come back home. Momma herded us back into our yard while Dad went to meet the little boy.

I heard Dad say, "Your Dad didn't kill your Momma, son. There she is, coming to get you."

We all turned around. She was all bent over and sobbing as she stumbled up the road. She had one hand on her head and one on her ribs. Momma and Dad went to meet her. They held her between them, brought her up and set her down in a rocking chair on the porch. She was crying and sobbing something awful.

Suddenly, she got real silent, looked up at Daddy and said, "God forgive me, I done shot Jake dead."

Every one of us children slammed our palms over our mouths in surprise. Momma began praying.

"Now Mary, you sit right here and I will go check on Jake. Maybe you just hurt him bad," Dad said.

He nodded to my oldest brother and they ran down to the house. They entered the house and didn't come out for a long, long time. One by one all my brothers went down to the house. I got up my nerve and started down there myself. Half way down my brother came out to meet me.

"She shot him good," he said. "She shot right through his heart. He is dead."

As Dad walked out the front door, I approached the back porch door. The house had settled and was slanted backward towards the back porch. The back screen door was wide open and there was dead Jake right before my eyes.

This is what I heard happened. He had beaten Mary all weekend, accusing her of running around on him while he was gone. He had hit one of the boys with an iron that made a dent in his forehead that looked like a perfect crease. He surely had a concussion, but no one seemed to notice. Of course, Jake had been drunk all weekend. Around noon that day, he told Mary he was going to sit down in a chair and take a nap.

Jake said, "When I wake up I am going to beat you some more. I'm going to beat you until I beats the evil out of you." Then he sat down in a straight-backed chair, leaned it back against the wall and passed out cold.

Only a dumb drunk would expect a woman to wait around for a beating. Maybe he had forgotten about the 12-gauge shotgun Bob had given to Mary, but she hadn't forgotten.

She must have been awfully close when she shot him because she blew his chest wide open. She blew his chair half out the back door and laid the chair and Jake plumb backwards half in the house and half on the porch. What was left of his body was still sitting in the chair. I am sure he never knew what hit him. It was going to take an awful scrubbing to get the mess cleaned up.

I just stood there dumbstruck; Jake's blood was running off the porch, it was making a little puddle on the stepping-stone and the hound that slept under their house was licking it up.

When I got used to the scene, I kept daring my brothers to touch him. But, no one, including me, went any closer to Jake Bain.

Soon, we heard the sheriff's siren. Now I don't know how the news spread, but everyone living within five miles showed up at the same time. There was a line of cars behind the sheriff and they all got out at once. My Dad met the sheriff and the crowd gathered around them. We knew we weren't supposed to be there. We took off running like scared rabbits back to our house.

Ivy Aaron Barnes

The News Spread Like Fire

People just kept coming. Kids came across the fields and down the road on their bikes. They propped their bikes on the tree trunks and climbed up to watch from the limbs. There were white folks also. The first white folks to arrive were Mr. William and Miss Jo Rozzelle. Then Annie Beth and Jeff Nixon drove up in their Buick. I guess it was a community tragedy and everyone came. The men walked up to the house. I could see my dad, Mr. Nixon and Mr. Will Rozzelle talking with the sheriff.

The Sheriff and my dad walked up to our house to talk with Mary. We scattered again, but this time we climbed up in the trees with the other kids.

There was an awful lot of moving around in the yard of the house. The people were huddled in groups. Other white folks arrived. Then the men folks, black and white, got together and started talking. But it was the women that I watched. G-G, Henrietta and Jenny walked with the white women up to our house. The women were walking fast and looking upset.

Mary was still sitting on the porch. She wasn't hollering any more, but she kept waving her apron in the air and covering her face with it. The women pulled the porch chairs over and gathered round her. It looked like everyone was talking at the same time.

More folks came down the road. All our neighbors, black and white were gathering. Mr. Tad Rozzelle drove up, got out of his car, lit up one of his cigars and walked inside the Bain house.

Some men followed him inside. Mr. Will and Mr. Tad covered Jake's body with a sheet, but they didn't move the chair out from under him. Then all the men walked up the hill toward the women folks.

I didn't know it then, but the sheriff was going to arrest Mary and take her to jail. When he got to the porch and tried to arrest Mary, the women weren't about to let that happen. They started shouting and shaking their fingers. The men just stood there. There was some powerful arguing going on, but we couldn't hear from the tree what they were saying. Some of us went back to the house to see if we could hear what was going on inside.

When we walked through the crowds at the road, I heard Mr. Cooper and Mr. Wallen talking.

"Jake was a good man when he wasn't drinking. He was a hard worker." Virgil Cooper said. "But I ain't never seen a meaner drunk."

"Hell," Hank Wallen replied, "last time I saw him he was doing some plowing for me and he had started drinking. I didn't know it until I saw him beating my best mule. He almost killed that mule. I never hired him again. You can't ruin a good working animal. Jake was a mean drunk."

We got into the house and sneaked into the front room. I heard the women arguing with the sheriff. "Mary is sick and you are not going to take her to jail," Mrs. Nixon was practically screaming.

Mama and Miss Jo were squatting on each side of Mary. I heard Miss Jo ask, "Mary, did he beat you all weekend?"

"Yes."

"Look, there is blood all over her dress," Miss Jo pointed out to the sheriff.

"The law is the law," the sheriff answered.

"Sheriff, let's walk a bit and talk this over," Mr. William asked.

"Let's go look in the house and see if we don't find signs of a fight," Mr. Tad said.

Every man down by the road joined them as they walked back to the Bain house.

The women sounded like cackling crows.

"They can't take this sick woman to jail."

"She needs to be in the hospital."

"If a man ever deserved to be shot it was Jake Bain."

"Where do you hurt, Mary?"

"Where are your children?"

"I'll go get them out of that tree and take them to my house."

"We got to do something to keep this poor woman out of jail."

"I hate to break the law."

"Drunks kill women all the time. No one goes to jail when that happens."

"We need to send someone to tell her sisters."

"I heard tell he killed her baby this spring."

"Where did he get his liquor?"

"I think he has a still nearby."

"We'll find it and destroy it."

"Don't say anything to the sheriff."

"We have got to get Mary to the hospital."

The men were walking back towards the house.

"Looks like there was a powerful struggle down there," the sheriff said.

"Yeah, I believe she shot him to save the family," Mr. Tad added.

"He was coming at you with a knife, wasn't he, Mary?" the sheriff asked.

"We found one on the kitchen floor," Mr. William said.

The women and Mary were suddenly quiet.

"She needs to go to the hospital," one of the women said. "She could be bleeding internally."

Finally, the sheriff spoke. "I can't see any reason to call this anything but a bad case of self defense. And I don't think we need to take anyone to jail. Especially since Mary is in bad need of going to the hospital." All the women looked at each other.

"Virgil Cooper and his wife are going to take Mary to St. Samaritan Hospital and leave her there. Rev. Aaron and some of the men are going to bury Jake down in the graveyard by his parents," continued the Sheriff.

"I'll give him a nice Christian burial," my dad assured everyone.

"Now let us all go home and have a nice Sunday afternoon," stated the sheriff.

Daisy Aaron Black

The Funeral

It took a while, but everyone left. Dad let all the children attend the funeral. Hardly anybody else stuck around for the service. It was a short service with Dad referring to forgiveness a lot. After that day, we never saw Mary or her kids again. And we never spoke of the killing again. We were told to forget what happened and to pray for Jake and Mary's souls that, but that was all. I heard tell that Mary and her kids went to live with a sister in Tennessee. It all happened a long time ago, but I think they handled it right. Jake was a mean drunk.

Ivy Aaron Barnes

Mary Bain Goes To The Hospital

They bundled Mary up in blankets, put a towel around her head and sat her in my car. I could smell blood the whole ride to the hospital. We didn't say one word the whole way to the hospital. I just did not know what to say after I told her I was sorry about what happened. My wife rode in the back of the car with Mary. We just dropped her off at the front desk and left.

I took my wife to the hospital the next day to check on Mary. But I waited in the car. My wife told me her sister was in the room with her and the doctor had been there too. Turns out Mary had three broken ribs, a concussion, and had a miscarriage during the night. Sounded like she had been in pretty bad shape, if she had not killed him, my guess is he would have killed her.

I forget what happened after that. Someone said she went to live with her sister. New folks eventually moved into the old house. I believe they were white folks.

Zeke Cooper

Jenny Grant Marries

Jenny Grant married for the first time at the age of seventy-five. The groom was seventy-eight. He drove them to York, South Carolina for the ceremony. When they drove home that night and told the news to Jenny's sisters, G-G and Henrietta, they were furious. G-G got so furious she grabbed her toothbrush and moved in with Henrietta that very night.

The houses were so close together, the women hollered good night to each other through the open windows in the summertime. "That old man just married Jenny so he would have someone to take care of him," they told everyone in Shuffletown.

This opinion did not seem to bother Jenny or her husband. Jenny went about her chores and cooked their meals. The husband just mostly sat on the front porch he seemed happy. On Mondays, Wednesdays and Fridays, Jenny walked up to William Rozzelle's house to clean and cook him a good meal. In the afternoon when William drove Jenny home, the men would sit on the porch and visit.

It was a short marriage. Jenny's husband died after a year and a half. G-G moved back in with Jenny and things returned to normal.

Judy Rozzelle

Old Maids?

People used to ask Mary and me why we never got married. Well, we never dated much. I always answered that we were never unhappy just being at home. We were just two content sisters and never thought of ourselves as Old Maids.

Iris Wallace

71

The Wallace Women

I was told by folks that the Abernethy women didn't ever marry cause they couldn't find a man who could fix a fence as good as they could.

Lee Wallace

Marriage Did Not Agree With Yvonne

Yvonne Johnson Herbert married twice for a combined total of eleven months. Her first marriage lasted ten months. Ten years later, she married again. This time it was a church wedding, but she was back home in a month. It was over before I even bought her a present. I have forgotten what his name was.

Yvonne could make up her mind quickly. She just did not believe in stewing about things. "A mistake is a mistake," she would say, "no matter how you look at it. And it is best to get out before it gets messy."

Judy Rozzelle

Judy Liked Wearing Wedding Dresses

When it came to men, Judy didn't have the good sense God gave a goat and to make it worse she had the attention span of a hummingbird. She drove me crazy. When I took her out and introduced her, I'd say, "This is Cousin Judy, she hasn't got a lick of sense, but she's got big boobs." Judy could get married 100 times to the jackasses of her choice. But I always knew she'd return to Shuffletown as assuredly as spring turns to summer.

Yvonne Rozzelle Herbert

Vernon And Smiley

Back around 1880, Andrew Rozzelle tells his deaf son, Vernon, that he has met a hog farmer in Waxhaw who has a deaf daughter named Smiley. Vernon gets in his wagon and rides off to meet her. A week later, he comes home with Smiley as his wife. They have five children two are mute and three are not. William Alexander Rozzelle, Sr. was the eldest son and he was not a mute. He became Pop-Pop's father and Will Rozzelle, my husband's grandfather.

William was sixteen when his sister Sarah was born. The second son, Dan, who was also not mute, had died about three years earlier. The other two children, Mary and Jeff, were mutes. I guess William was always silent in the house and always used sign language to talk to the family. And I guess Sarah was a very good baby because Sarah was almost two when someone heard her calling one of the cousins by name at the big house. Until that time, everyone thought Sarah was a mute also.

Barbara Gillis Rozzelle

Elizabeth McMillan Rozzelle

When Andrew Rozzelle married Elizabeth McMillan, she was fourteen and still playing with dolls. When she was an old woman, she kept her pockets full of pennies to give to the children. But she never stopped watching the road north, hoping to see her sons return from the Civil War.

Anne Rozzelle Griffin

Living In The Chicken House

I had to move into the chicken coop. The house just wasn't big enough for both of us. Jennifer and I were arguing or disagreeing about something darn near all the time, and there's only so much a man can take. It wasn't so bad living in the chicken house.

Fifteen hundred chickens used to live in it, so it was plenty big. I built a wall at the back end to make a large room, about fifteen by fifteen. The room had three big windows. I kept a big old kerosene heater and a small one too, an air compressor, and a propane tank for my grill in the chicken house. I had to add two air conditioners come summer 'cause those coops can get awful hot. But I was comfortable. And it was quiet down there.

In fact, my TV got better reception in there than it did in the main house. I didn't have a telephone, and I didn't want one. I would have probably stayed there for a long time, maybe the rest of my life, but see this sunk-in place on my head?

This caused me to have to move back into the house. My tractor got stuck while I was out grading a field, so I put this big old board under one of the tires to get me some traction. Well, it flew out and damn near killed me.

Jennifer took me back in the house and cared for me or I might have died. It's funny, though. No sooner did I get better than she up and died.

Bill Short

Love At First Sight

I fell in love with Floyd Greene the first time I saw him. It was at a little country store across the river—a place we hung out every now and then. It had a jukebox and that drew us there to dance. On that day, Floyd and his brother, Edward, stopped in the store on their way home to South Carolina.

I already knew Edward, so I asked who it was he had with him. Edward said, "This is my brother, Floyd." Floyd's hair was coal black, his eyes were dark brown, and he had a great smile. He had on a starched green and white shirt. Standing right there, in that moment, I fell in love with Floyd Greene.

I started looking for him at the Saturday night square dances they held in the commissary building where Floyd worked. He always asked me to dance. He was always dressed neat and proper. We did not go around in sloppy clothes back then. One night when the dance was over, Floyd asked me if he could come by to see me. "I reckon so," I answered.

One Sunday, Floyd and Edward were returning from a weekend at their Mom's in South Carolina and Floyd asked for a lift to see someone that night. Edward said he was also going out that evening and he would be glad to drop Floyd off. As they approached my Dad's house, my brother and I were standing in the yard. Edward blew his horn and waved. Floyd said, "That's the girl I'm going to see tonight." "Oh, no," Edward moaned, "That's where I was going." Floyd and I were married six months later.

Ollie Greene

Kissing Leads To Marriage

My bedroom was on the second floor of our house. I spent many nights staring out across the dark road and onto the Gillis's front porch.

Once this vigilance paid off. I saw Annie Beth Gillis kiss Jeff Nixon goodnight after a date. Later on, Annie Beth and Jeff married, moved down the road, built a brick house, and began their family. For a long time I thought that if you kissed someone, you had to marry him.

Judy Rozzelle

Ollie's Chocolate Syrup Cake

One of my family's favorite desserts is my chocolate syrup cake. I served it the first time around the holidays and every now and then, I still make it today. It is gooey and good. You shouldn't eat more than a couple of pieces after dinner. This is the recipe and it may not be right. My memory is not what it used to be. But I think I can get it all in my mind.

You need a one-pound can of chocolate syrup, like the kind you put on ice cream and one cup of sugar or is it two cups of sugar? No, I am sure you only need one cup of sugar. Pour the sugar and the syrup into a mixing bowl with four eggs and one stick of melted butter, a teaspoon of baking powder and one cup of flour. You mix it all up until it is smooth and creamy. Then bake it in a long pan at 325 degrees until it is done. I still test my cake with a straw, but sometimes I run a knife through the middle to tell if it is done.

To make the icing you need two cups of sugar, one-half cup of milk, one teaspoon of vanilla and one-quarter cup of cocoa. You cook it in a pot on top of the stove on low heat until it comes to a boil. You only boil it for a minute and you have to put it on the cake before it hardens. It doesn't matter if the cake has cooled or not. The frosting will harden.

Another thing my family loves is pizza burgers. It is a good quick meal. I started serving it in the 60s and I still make it today. You need to mix up ground chuck. Don't get ground round, it doesn't have enough fat. You dice an onion and mix it all together with a whole lot of ketchup. Then you open the hamburger buns and brown them under the broiler. When they are nice and brown, you place a slice of tomato on the bun. Then you put the mixture all over the toasted bun and broil it for about seven minutes. Just before you take it out of the oven, you add a piece of cheese on top, if you want to.

I am a good cook, but I was never much on keeping house. I made a home for my family that they liked to return to at the end of the day.

Ollie Greene

Sister Anne Falls In Love

I believe my sister Anne fell in love with Rob Griffin because his eyes were as blue as our grandfather's eyes. Poppa's eyes were blue as a Carolina sky. They were so clear you could almost see right through them. Yes, that was the first thing that attracted Anne to Rob Griffin.

Let me assure you, she did not fall in love with him because of his car. At sixteen, Rob drove the smallest car ever designed with an engine. Most other cars that small are filled with kids hollering, "*Brrrooom, Brrrooom.*" It was a 1959 Metropolitan. It looked like a very large black and white brogan shoe, size 23.

Or, it could have been a used clown car left behind by a carnival. It made Volkswagens look spacious.

They were both skinny and tall, Rob was six feet four inches tall and Anne would admit to five feet ten inches. When Rob picked her up for a date and he held the door while she folded up and bent down into the car. I sometimes watched to see if their heads would pop out the roof or if their legs would punch out the headlights. It was like watching two walking stick insects squeeze into a little Bayer Aspirin tin and driving it off.

Ten days after Anne turned nineteen, she announced that she was marrying Rob Griffin on Saturday, ten days before he was to set sail with the United States Navy. Her announcement gave Mom and Dad ten days to plan the wedding. There were three bridesmaids, with me as maid of honor. The night before the wedding there was the usual rehearsal and cake cutting. I expected baby shower invitations to follow in the next ten weeks.

She and Mom made most of the yellow empress style bridesmaid dresses that were flocked with daisies and we carried daisy bouquets. Anne always loved daisies, but what I did not know was that daisies were a big deal to Anne because once upon a time, Rob Griffin ate daisies.

I guess he learned to do that when he was spending so much time tied to the clothesline with a calf. Rob has often told me that that cow was his first pet, but I think the cow considered Rob a pet. I'm just surprised he doesn't still munch on daisies.

We first noticed Rob's eccentricities the first Christmas after they were married when he came home on leave. At that time, he was one of many breakfast cooks on the USS Roosevelt and his job was to fry soft eggs. Mom was the only one who ate soft eggs, but on that Christmas morning, we all did, and so did anyone who had the misfortune to stop by.

And he sent home photos of himself that made Anne run to her bedroom exclaiming, "What have I done?" In the photos, Rob would have his hair sticking out all over his head with his finger near an electrical socket. In other photos, he would have a wrench in his mouth pulling his teeth. According to his letters, he was the practical joker on the ship. Anne looked at those photos and said, "Somebody is gonna kill that idiot before they get to Vietnam."

I guess Rob did not show any potential as a cook or he stuck his finger in a socket one too many times, because he was transferred from the *USS Roosevelt* to the *USS Saratoga*. On the *USS Saratoga*, Rob was assigned to the communications division and the ship sailed for the Mediterranean. The Seven Day War started and they did not let Bob off the boat for two months. That was probably a good idea.

Judy Rozzelle

Rob Griffin Passes Out At The Sight Of Blood

If Rob has to go to see a doctor and they need to draw blood, I tell them they had better lay him down on something before they draw blood, or they will have to get a 200-pound man off the floor. Some doctors don't listen the first time, but they always listen the second time.

Anne Rozzelle Griffin

Rob Stops Smoking

It got a little tricky around the Griffin household when Rob Griffin gave up smoking and took to chewing tobacco. Anne considered this new habit repulsive and should only be practiced away from home. But Rob came home every night, collapsed into his BarcaLounger and spit in a Styrofoam cup, which he put on the kitchen counter when he headed for bed.

The debate must have gone something like this.

"Rob, please don't do that?"

The second week... "Rob, stop spitting and throw those nasty cups away!"

The third week into the habit... "Take those nasty cups off my kitchen counter. I'd rather you kept smoking. Now, I'm gonna have to kill you."

Four weeks and one night into his new addiction, Rob picked up Anne's cup filled with Pepsi and spit in it. I have not been able to pin Anne down on what exactly happened after this accident.

Finally, she says she decided that if he was going to have such a stupid habit, she would never touch those vile cups filled with tobacco spit.

At the end of the first week, the end table by Rob's chair was loaded with the vile cups and each cup was filled to the brim.

She told me he thought she was joking.

At this point, she must have started sleeping on the couch, for they reached a compromise. Rob would continue to chew tobacco, but Anne would never be responsible for disposing of those nasty Styrofoam cups.

For years when I'd visit my sister in her immaculately clean home, it was always startling to pass her kitchen counter, where he kept his spit cups until he remembered to dispose of them. Sometimes, there were twelve to sixteen cups of chewed tobacco lined up on the far corner of the counter.

"I am not taking those nasty things out," she would explain. "He'll get them in his own time."

Rob would tell any who inquired that the cups were a science experiment for rose mulch. Then Anne would add, "I don't have to have the Ladies' Bible Study at home this year. There's always something to be thankful for."

Judy Rozzelle

Sister Judy

I could handle being married to Rob Griffin easily because of my sister Judy. I just went from living with one odd person, Judy, to living with another one.

Anne Rozzelle Griffin

Dad Steps Over Rob

I was down at Anne's one night talking to her while she made supper. Suddenly, Rob ran in the back door hollering, "Damnit, I cut myself."

Before he could say another word, he keeled over onto the floor of the utility room. Anne walked over and saw it was just his finger and went back to peeling potatoes.

Daddy came in the back door about that time. He rang the back door bell and came on inside like we all did back then. He had to step over Rob's body to get to the kitchen. He sat down on a stool took off his hat, and asked how we were as usual. But every now and then, he would look over in the direction where Rob was lying.

Finally, he asked, "Should we do something about him?"

"He'll be all right," Anne answered as she sliced potatoes into a pan. "He'll come to in time to eat."

"Well, don't let the children jump on him," Daddy advised.

Judy Rozzelle

My Tombstone

Rob has promised me he will put on my tombstone the words, "She Tried. God knows she tried." Now if he dies first, I will leave instructions to further note on my tombstone, "She lived with Rob Griffin for however many years it turns out to be."

Anne Rozzelle Griffin

Patience, Love And Marriage

Anne Griffin loves her husband, Rob, and she has never found much to complain about. But she often sighs with acceptance and exasperation. Many, many times, she has looked at me and said, "Well, what else can I do?" Then she smiles gets in the car to go home and fix supper. Like most married folks around Shuffletown, she was happily married and accepted that life was not supposed to be perfect.

Judy Rozzelle

Institutions, Tradition and Other Curiosities

Tradition And Sweet Potato Cobbler

It was always a tradition in my family to take down the Christmas tree on the first day of January and burn it. Then we set down to a meal of peas, cornbread and collard greens. There was a barrel of dried peas in the barn. To fix the peas we scooped them out of the barrel and soaked them overnight. Then they were set to cooking right after breakfast. We ate them that night. We burned pinewood in the cook stove and burned hard wood such as oak to heat the house.

Sweet potatoes and Irish potatoes were dug up in the summer time and stored under a layer of straw in the root cellar. This would keep them all winter. When we wanted some potatoes, we would dig them out and cook them up.

Corn was kept in the corncrib. When we wanted corn, we pulled it out and shucked it. The best corn was taken to the mill for grinding. There was not a fee for grinding meal. You paid a toll and that meant the miller kept a certain amount of the ground meal.

The cornmeal was stored in stone jars with the canned jars of food on shelves in the basement. There were rows and rows of jars filled with black berries, peaches, string beans, tomatoes and they tasted good all winter, all from last summer's garden. When it got real cold, Dad would go down by Long Creek and gather the limbs of the spicewood tree. We cut the limbs up and Mama would make steaming spicewood tea.

Winter and fall are the seasons to set rabbit boxes and hunt rabbits. You don't hunt rabbits in the summer months when rabbits have a wobble. Pregnant rabbits have big stomachs and walk with a wobble. Winter is the time to hunt rabbits. A feast was a pan of rabbits in brown gravy, cooking on a wood burning stove, and flat bread. Flat bread was biscuit dough rolled out in a pan and cooked in the oven. I don't remember a day when we went hungry. There were 15 kids, but my dad was an excellent hunter. Sometimes when the snow was the deepest and the winter the coldest, we ate the best.

Mama used to bake a cobbler dish out of sweet potatoes for Christmas, Thanksgiving and special Sunday dinners that I still bake today. It was a family favorite back then and it still is decades later.

Mama knew secrets about herbs, spices and cooking on a wood stove. Still, I think my recipe is as good as hers. I adapted the recipe with some ingredients that Mama didn't have back then, but it is still just as good as when Mama baked it. I'll give you the recipe.

Sweet Potato Cobbler

4 large sweet potatoes
4 cups sugar
2 tablespoons flour
1 teaspoon cinnamon
4 tablespoons vanilla butternut flavoring
1 ½ cups water
2 ½ pie crusts
2 sticks butter

Peel the potatoes and cut into thin slices. Lay the slices evenly in a 10" by 14" by 2" pan. Spread sugar, flour, cinnamon and flavoring over the top of the dish. Add water and shake the pan to blend the ingredients. Break or cut the piecrusts into pieces and place on top of the potatoes. Slice the butter and distribute it over the crusts. Bake at 400 degrees for one hour or until it is done and crust is brown. Serves 12 to 14 people.

Daisy Aaron Black

The Chapel

In the fall of 1887, when the air was sweet with the smell of hay, people donated mules, lumber, labor and time to build a one-room chapel. When the chapel was completed, it wasn't much to look at, just a square clapboard building standing on a strong stone foundation. Inside, the pulpit was like a bay window with the stage extending four to five feet into the sanctuary. The pews were hand-hewn benches. This was the Lord's house and beauty blessed its plain exterior. Season followed season, rolling the years away and the chapel among the trees settled easily into the land and into the community. Reverend Sloan, the circuit minister, came at two p.m. each Sunday to preach the sermon. This chapel built by farmers became Sloan Memorial Methodist Church.

Judy Rozzelle

Horse Corn

My father was born in Ohio, and I can still hear people asking: "Y'all ain't from around here, are ye?" But he was thoroughly committed to living in the South and our place was his little bit of heaven. Every inch of it was used to plant something beautiful or useful. When it came time to plant corn, he planted the corn he knew, a hybrid called Country Gentleman. The neighbors watched in amusement as the Yankee plowed his field and planted his corn.

The old-timers chuckled behind their church bulletins. Everyone knew that by the Fourth of July the corn stalks should be as high as an elephant's eye. Their corn was. But my father's corn was just chest level when the ears began to get shriveled brown tassels, indicating they were ready to pick.

So, at the church picnic that Sunday, my father presented a huge covered dishful of his corn. My mother had stayed at home to cook it fresh off the stalk so it would be hot enough to melt the sweet country butter. His corn was yellow, theirs was white, and so they were suspicious until that first bite. Daddy's corn was heaven on a cob the farmers and their wives agreed on that. And the following year, Country Gentleman had its proud place in most Shuffletown gardens. What I knew, and what we never told the neighbors, was that Daddy called the tall-stalked, white variety: "Horse corn."

Gail E. Haley

Rozzelle Ferry

The Abernethys operated the first ferry across the Catawba River. In 1840, Richard Andrew Rozzelle and his family bought the ferry and many acres of land from the Abernethys.

"We're not sure when the original Rozzelle House was built. We know some of it was built in 1849, but parts of it were older. Aunt Judy insists it was renovated in 1849.

"The last time I know of Rozzelle Ferry operating was after the great Catawba River Flood in 1916. The flood washed the bridge out as well as most of the bridges. I don't know how long it took them to rebuild the bridge, but it was several years and the Rozzelle Family pulled out the old ferry and once again ferried people to the other side.

"What fascinates me is how the area has changed. Now you don't live on the river, you live on the lake. In fact, it is now called Mt. Island

Lake, not the Catawba River, and it is now a prestigious thing to live on the lake.

"When I was growing up, people bought two or three acres along the river, hauled in a trailer and called it their river place. Now, they build expensive homes on small lots and chop down all the trees. Usually they have finely manicured lawns, which require chemicals and fertilizers and more asphalt stuff that is not good for the river or the land."

Frank Rozzelle

Coming Home

When the car approached home from the northwest, just as Dad drove the car to the top of the hill where the old Hilltop Service Station set, you could see the crossroads and you could see our house. I always sat up at this time and looked over Mother's shoulder in the front seat. Below lay the crossroads of Shuffletown. On the right was Uncle Tad's Shuffletown Grocery. Settled solidly in the corner of the crossroads was the towering oak tree by the Gaines sisters' front yard.

And just beyond the crossroads was home. I could see a driveway leading into a cover of oak trees. We were almost there. This circle of tree tops with their boughs huddled together like umbrellas in a rainstorm wreathed the entrance to our house. Beneath this deep green of summer, beneath the gold of autumn and the winter ribs, sat home, safe harbor. Seeing home and knowing the porch light is always on, calls to the soul like sunset. Having a place, belonging, is a primal need at any age.

Judy Rozzelle

Duke's Television And Repair Shop

In 1953, Duke Roundtree opened Duke's Television and Repair Shop inside the old Spurrier gas station. The store was tiny and dark with a dirty floor. Duke would try to fix anything, but his expertise was radios and black-and-white televisions. He was always sitting behind the tall counter on a high stool working on something, like a bartender polishing a glass while waiting on thirsty customers.

The moment you stepped through the door, he looked up and said, "Hey there," as if he had been expecting you. His smile always reminded me of the Cheshire cat in *Alice in Wonderland*. Duke was always good for a laugh and a little gossip. He did have the best view of the crossroads from that stool. Some folks around these parts thought he could tell the future. I think he just knew when to talk and when to listen.

Lined up on the shelves behind him were toasters, waffle irons, rotary fans and black-and-white TVs. Their cords were the old thick black kind woven with black thread.

Duke's prices to fix things always varied. You just left the appliance, and Duke would say it wouldn't be much, but to keep in mind that he charged an extra dollar for every time he got shocked fixing it.

There were so many things lined up in his store. Mostly he accumulated small appliances people had given up on ever running again, but just couldn't stand to throw away.

Barbara Gillis Rozzelle

Orson Welles Ate Supper At The Big House

"It's hard to be strangers with someone when you've just asked him to pass the delicious candied yams. The restaurant is in a century-old white frame house that sits at the foot of the Catawba River Bridge on Highway 16, ten miles north of Charlotte, North Carolina."

That was a commercial Orson Welles recorded for Eastern Airlines in 1971. He was talking about the atmosphere at the Rozzelle Ferry House.

Eastern Airlines developed the commercials that ran nationally to spotlight unique restaurants in Dallas, Chicago, St. Louis, New York City and Shuffletown. The commercial drew many visitors stopping over in Charlotte's airport out to the Rozzelle Ferry House to eat southern cooking family style.

There was always a mix of people sharing food at the long tables in the Rozzelle House. Fisherman, plumbers, executives and once, when he was passing through Charlotte, Orson Welles came out to check out the candied yams. Which he did. He ate a bunch of them and, it was reported, close to two whole fried chickens.

Tad Rozzelle

Newspaper Town

In a sense, Shuffletown was a newspaper town. The three Rozzelle Brothers left the farm and followed the written word.

Each one got a job working for the Charlotte newspapers and with the money saved from the newspaper jobs, they bought land at the crossroads in Shuffletown.

85

They delivered the news. They were route carriers and they delivered the newspapers out into the country to the rural folk. In myth and in memory, in the days of King Arthur and Queen Victoria, bringing the news was a sacred trust. And the Rozzelle brothers were committed to this trust. William Rozzelle, my dad, was first to get a job on the newspaper. When he was sixteen, Chancy Stephens hired him to deliver the *Charlotte News*.

Each day he drove Mr. Stephens's car downtown to the *Charlotte News* Building on College Street and drove behind the building to the loading dock, where barrels of black ink and bundled newspapers waited for delivery. Some days, he arrived early and entered into the shadowed rooms with high overhead lights, where men in ink-stained aprons operated groaning printing presses. These men held the finished product, the day's newspaper, while it was still warm like homemade bread.

Next, his brother Tad found a job at the *Charlotte News*. Years later when the youngest brother, Harrison, turned sixteen, he followed his brothers into the newspaper business. Harrison still remembers the day William stopped and told him there was a job opening at the paper.

"I had spent the morning, steadying the plow and hollering at our stubborn old mule. It was 1936, and a job was a blessing. I borrowed my dad's car, a Hudson Whippet, and began delivering newspapers in the afternoon and plowing fields in the morning."

In those years, they delivered the newspapers on washboard dirt roads that ran deep with red mud when it rained and froze hard in winter. When the roads were impassable, men on horseback met them to receive the papers.

Tad Rozzelle told of one hill on the road to Gastonia that a car loaded with Sunday newspapers couldn't climb without stalling out...unless you were driving backwards. This involved sticking your head out of the window, prayerfully looking backwards while balancing the forces between the clutch and accelerator, and steadying the steering wheel with one hand. Every Sunday, Uncle Tad executed this feat successfully. He would turn his car around, gun the motor and assault the hill. When the road leveled out, he turned his car around and continued on to Gastonia.

When World War II exploded in Hawaii, all three brothers went into town to enlist and they were away from home overnight. There were no telephones in Shuffletown; their wives thought they had enlisted, and would be far away before they heard from them again. But the next morning, they came home upset. They had been exempted from the army because their job was delivering newspapers.

Their territory included west Charlotte, Gastonia, Stanley, Marion and Lincolnton. They hired carriers and mapped out their routes. If the cars broke down, which they often did, their wives took the kids, picked up the carrier and helped him finish delivering the paper.

Tossing a folded newspaper out of a moving car while holding onto the steering wheel and hitting the target with any degree of accuracy is an art. The artist, the seasoned carrier, could toss a rolled newspaper over the top of a moving car and hit the center of a front porch or at least a nearby tree without taking his eyes off the road.

During those years, they delivered newspapers to everyone who could afford to subscribe, and many who couldn't. If people could not afford the newspaper they bartered. Ears of corn, chickens, and buckets of coal were all currency.

A farmer once offered Tad Rozzelle a pig for a newspaper subscription. Tad didn't have a truck and a loose pig in the backseat of his car was simply not acceptable. He convinced his brother-in-law, Austin, to ride with him to get the pig. They stuck the pig in a feed sack and with the promise of bacon, he persuaded Houston to hold the squealing pig in the back seat for the trip home. On this afternoon, he discovered that a car that can't climb the hill loaded with Sunday newspapers…also can't climb the hill carrying a pig in a poke and a frantic passenger.

One subscriber who lived near Stanley fell behind on his bill. He kept promising my Dad he would pay the next week. Dad kept paying for the man's subscription, but the money owed became too much. One day, Dad drove to Stanley. He was going to cancel the man's subscription. They stood in the man's front yard, and the man must have thought he was about to lose his newspaper.

"Walk around back with me," he said to Dad. In the corner of the porch sat a wringer washing machine.

"What about trading me the news for the washing machine?" the man asked.

"We might could work something out," Dad said, "But what would your wife say if you traded her new washing machine for the newspaper?"

"It'll be all right with her," the man replied. "Yesterday, she caught her hair in the wringers."

Judy Rozzelle

87

The Minnow Pools

Uncle Tad always had an idea, and most of them made money. When he grew tired of repairing cars, he took out the grease rack beside Shuffletown Grocery and turned the grease pit into two deep cement ponds. Each cement pond was narrow, deep and painted sky blue on the inside. He filled the cement ponds with minnows where they swam in layers until they were scooped out and sold.

They were as deep as Uncle Tad was tall. We used to watch him stand in them to scrub them out. You could tap on his head if you had the nerve. The idea worked. It was not long before fishermen heading for the Catawba River for a day of fishing stopped at Shuffletown Grocery for a pail or two of minnows.

One day a man drove up, parked his car, got out and walked past the little screened-in room Uncle Tad had built around the minnow ponds. He heard the water churning. He went in to see what was going on and became intrigued by the layers and layers of little fish swimming about in the narrow ponds. He must have knelt down for a closer look, which caused him to lose his balance for he tumbled into a pond.

Uncle Tad came out of the store hollering, "Get out, you can't bathe in there."

Yvonne Herbert Rozzelle

Reese Cleghorn, *The Charlotte Observer,* March 1976
Shuffletown Grocery Calendar

If you planned to head out to the Shuffletown Gro., buy some minnows and fish in the Catawba River today, you'd better hold up until you read this. The fishing guide on the Shuffletown Gro. Calendar is two-thirds wrong.

Each day on the calendar has a small drawing of a fish. A white fish indicates good fishing. I thought this was a fine public service. But now I am having to revise every page of my calendar.

Reese Cleghorn

The Calendar Is Wrong

We got it reversed. Where the white fish shows it ought to be a good fishing day, it really is a bad day for fishing. And where it shows a poor fishing day, it is really a good day to go fishing. We did get a few days right. The days marked for fair fishing are right. The calendar says today is a good fishing day and that means it's poor. So, I won't charge you for the minnows. Next year, we are going to get the calendar right. It sure has been a headache this year. Then, again, we probably won't even do a calendar next year. You just stop by here and ask what kind of day it is to fish.

Tad Rozzelle

Uncle Tad Knew What He Liked

Uncle Tad preferred workshirts for the store. He liked to wear a khaki work shirt and a cotton undershirt. The cotton undershirt was what the movie star, Bob Mitchum, wore in movies when he was shaving or about to kick butt.

Aunt Mabe once, in a flight of fancy, bought him an attractive knit shirt to wear at the store. Some time that day, a customer came in and complimented his shirt. Uncle Tad took it off and gave it to him. That was the last knit shirt she ever bothered to buy him. However, she did remind him often of the shirt he gave away.

Judy Rozzelle

Judy Is High Strung

Cousin Judy was filling her car with gas one afternoon at the store. I sneaked up behind her, stuck my finger against her back and blew in her ear. I do not recall exactly what occurred next, but when all the hollering and stomping was over, I had gas on my clothes. Judy was jumping up and down, hollering like a stuck pig and pointing the gas nozzle at me like a gun.

Whatever happened sure entertained the folks in the store. At least seven people were staring out the window laughing. Judy was still stomping her feet about five minutes later. She is a little high strung. Have you noticed that? What can I say, she is a Rozzelle? I am just glad she didn't strike a match.

Cotton Henderson

Mac Gillis, My Granddaddy

It used to worry Grandpa that Dottie and I didn't eat a lot of candy. Truth is, our Daddy had scared us to death about eating too much sugar and losing our teeth. But Grandpa did not understand. "He would say, "Your Grandpa owns a candy store and you don't eat candy."

I remember the night his store burned. We stood on the porch and watched the flames. Grandpa fell and cut his chin trying to get inside the store to retrieve some of Grandmother's stuff he treasured and kept in his safe, but the fire was too hot and he didn't save anything. Grandpa was never the same after the store burned. He seemed forever sad after that day. He "kept company," as my mom and Aunt Doe said, with a Mrs. Spurrier. They liked her, and always wished Grandpa had married her, but at least he had someone to go square dancing with. But after the fire, he went to live with Aunt Doe in Kings Mountain. That fire changed our lives forever. We got up one morning and the store was gone.

Sara Gillis

Miss Abbie's Chickens

There was a footpath to Miss Abbie's house just beyond my back porch and I loved to visit her. She was always baking something and her house always smelled like apples and cinnamon or baking bread.

When she got older, I made up excuses to visit her everyday so she would not suspect that I was checking up on her. I would ask her how to make soup, bake a roast or how to plant seeds. I came up with all kinds of things. One time I asked her how to sew a dart in a dress I was making. She must have thought I was the dumbest person she knew.

When she broke her arm, I told her I would feed the chickens. She said she didn't think her chickens would like a stranger feeding them. Nevertheless, I went down into the chicken yard and fed them every day at five o'clock. Miss Abbie said they liked to be fed at the same time every day.

In April, we set our clocks forward for Daylight Savings Time. I went over the next day at exactly five o'clock. The chickens were looking for me. They were lined up at the fence facing Miss Abbie's back porch. The moment they spied me coming down the path, they started squawking and cackling. They had expected their meal an hour earlier.

Marie Brafford

Miss Mamie And Miss Esther's Car

When I was working at Mack Gillis' service station, I had to go over to Miss Mamie and Miss Esther's once a month to gas up their car. I would knock on the door and one of them would hand me the key.

90

Then I would back the car out of the garage and on across the street to the station. They would need about a gallon of gas and I'd check their oil. The car was a 1950 Chevy. It was twelve years old and it might have had 200 miles on the odometer.

Rob Griffin

Homebody

I did not want to live anyplace else. I was in the Army reserves and that cured me of ever wanting to live anywhere else. I bought my girlfriend, Hazel, a house back in the late 80s and let her pay just a little rent until her boys grew up. Hazel and me kept company for more than twenty three years. I went over there most nights, but I came home to sleep. I loved my Mom and Dad and I just hated to leave them. Hazel was a good cook, but nobody cooked like Mom, and Dad needed someone to help him with the place. I always mowed the yard, plowed the garden and kept the pool clean. Figured I would take care of them when they got old. It was what I wanted to do.

Harry Rozzelle

The Gold Mine And Bootleggers

The old gold mine tunnel was right in the middle of our front yard. I finally took our tractors and covered it up with dirt. I spent all day doing it and then in the night, the mine tunnel collapsed. Could have been the end of me. Over the years, we had dumped all kinds of things down that shaft. Dad was the trash man around here for years, you know.

Nobody remembers when the mine was worked. All I remember is what grandmother told me. A fellow with Duke Power came out here a couple of years ago and got interested in it. He found enough gold to stamp out a piece about the size of a half dollar.

They had trouble keeping water out of the tunnel. They kept two pumps going all the time. One night the guard fell asleep; the pumps stopped and the tunnel flooded. There was also a fire once before that when the security guard fell asleep. I do know that they brought their gold up in buckets and there was this one man who came over and ran his fingers through the buckets to see how much gold they had. The guards started watching him and sure enough, he had long fingernails and he was collecting gold under his nails. He was clever...but not real clever.

I have heard tell that there are mine tunnels all around Shuffletown. It's a wonder nobody had fallen through one of those tunnels. This mine on our place was called the Dunn Mine. It was operating when they found that big nugget over at Reed Gold Mine. There was a mine over towards Plank Road and the Caps Hill mine on Peach Gut Holler in Oakdale. There is a Catholic mission over near Mt. Holly that was built for Irish miners when gold was hot around here. I think it's the oldest church in North Carolina.

I'm one of those fellas who never knew until tomorrow what they should have done yesterday. Like the banker president who built this house in 1903, he thought Duke Power was going to develop this area. He built about 100 years too soon.

The banker never lived out here, but he rented the house to one of his vice-presidents and that guy lived here for six months. He said he couldn't stand the mosquitoes out here and he moved back in town. He and the banker then built the area in Charlotte known as Dilworth.

My grandfather came out here and looked around. He wanted to buy the place, but he kept thinking about those mosquitoes. My grandmother said that if he would just go down to the creek and unclog the logs the mosquitoes would go away when the water started flowing. They bought the place, unclogged the logs and the mosquitoes went away...for the most part.

They used to run a little moonshine around here. Lots of folks kept their haystacks up there on the hill across the road. Some Scotsman had made a road of stone up there a long time ago before they built Rozzelles Ferry Road.

The old road was a good place to stack your hay. The stones kept it off the ground so the hay wouldn't rot. One night I was sitting up there with some other kids and this runner stopped his car in front of the haystacks then he ran over to one stack and pulled out a smoke screen? Do you know what a smoke screen is?

Well, they were screens filled with oil. Bootleggers put them over their carburetors and hooked them to a lever inside the car. If the cops spotted you, you pulled that lever and that slid the smoke screen in place. Oil started dropping into the engine and black smoke started rolling out your muffler. It didn't take long for the smoke from the oil to throw up a smoke screen. When that stuff got on the cop's windshield, he was out of the chase.

Another thing they did was to unhook their backlights so cops couldn't see where they were going. They also disconnected their front wheel brakes so they could brake without locking up. When the bootleggers did brake and pull off the road they could turn around and be gone before the cops could stop.

The police set up a roadblock down on Rozzelle Ferry Bridge one night and stopped a bootlegger. Somehow the bootlegger tipped his car and the moonshine fell into the river. The people in the village the other side heard the commotion. By the time the cops got to the river. The moonshine was gone down the river and they couldn't prosecute him.

Another time, somebody and me were hunting down on what was the old Davidson place and we found a still. We were about to inspect it when we heard a car and we hid. It was the cops with an axe and we watched them destroy the still. That was a close call. What had happened was a mill worker over in Mt. Holly had purchased a five-gallon jug of the stuff. He was drunk and pouring it into bottles on his front porch. The cops arrested him and asked him where he got it and he told them. Used to be a lot of things going on around here. It is a little tamer now.

Hank Wallen

The Shuffletown Drag Strip

In 1957, Nancy Fuller Hart and Larry Hart built a brick ranch home in what was once her father's watermelon patch by Long Creek. Saul Fuller bought the land adjoining Long Creek and the Wallen family in the early fifties. The Fullers were congenial with the Wallens for many years. For the most part both families got along.

One Sunday Mr. and Mrs. Eli Wallen called on Nancy, Larry and the elder Fullers. They sat down in the Harts' living room and Nancy offered everyone coffee. As she poured coffee, Eli Wallen, with his hat in his hand, explained how hard it was to make a living as a hardscrabble farmer.

"Times have not been good recently and it has been a pretty hard winter," he said. "Hank has an idea that might help support the family. He wants to start a drag racing track on the strip of land by Long Creek."

Hank Wallen had given his parents a bunch of trouble when he was growing up. Now, it seemed to the others that he was about to cause them and some other folks to experience this trouble. This would mean the cornfields by the creek would be plowed under and the roar of engines would fill the countryside.

The Fullers were mightily upset. Cows grazed in their pastures and drank from Long Creek. It was a beautiful, quiet stretch of land. It seemed drag racing in this area would be a sin. But they were torn between keeping the peace and being considerate of the Wallen family. They consulted the preacher, but it did not make much difference. The bulldozers arrived and the grading began on Eli Wallen's property within the week.

In the next four decades, fans parked on their lawns, climbed in their trees and traipsed through their property. Cars were sneaked into the drag strip at all hours of the night to drag race. Weekends were ruined and the cows were sold.

The Fullers and their neighbors began decades of legal battles with the Wallen Family. Shuffletown became a noisy place, and the Shuffletown Dragstrip became the area's largest tourist attraction.

Judy Rozzelle

Drag Racing

Dink Springer was the first to make money off drag racing. He had heard about the drag racing in Wisconsin. He decided he could do the same for the kids here. He scraped out a straight track on his farm in Pumpkin Center with his tractor. Kids mobbed the place and paid money to race. But his space was limited. One day, we were talking and he asked me about our land down there by Long Creek.

We were hardscrabble farmers who were tired of plowing and tired of hoping for good weather. So, we got a couple of bulldozers and leveled the land down there by the creek for racing. Kids were so excited about the racetrack that they started sneaking down there to race before we even finished grading. We had trouble from the get-go. The Fullers owned the pasture on the other side of Long Creek and they immediately complained about the noise.

Then we had complaints 'cause Saturday night races went on past midnight. The neighbors took us to court. The judge said we had to quit racing by 10 p.m. There was no way I could get those kids to shut down that early. I thought then that I was going to have to shut down. Then Dad suggested we move the drag races to Sunday. All we had to do was wait until one o'clock when the folks had gone home from church. We did all right for a while. We made more money on concessions than we did on racing.

We had some crazy times, some rabid fans and good cars. It was a good track. We did have one death. A guy was killed doing a flying stunt during intermission. He did the stunt one time and I paid him out of the concession money. He loved doing it so much he offered to do it again for free. We held up the racing, he got into position behind the car that was towing him down the track. They towed him until the wind caught his sails and carried him into the sky. But something happened after he had disengaged from the towline. He was high up there when his sails folded up. He fell like a rock. The crowd didn't make a noise. We had to shut down that day.

Drag racing is loud and we kept a lawyer busy. You wouldn't believe how much money I paid lawyers. Some lawyer was always working to keep us in business. Still, we made more money than we did farming. In the 70s, I leased the track and kept the concessions. When the city limits came out this way in the 80s, I got real tired of fighting the law and sold the whole place.

Hank Wallen

The Dragstrip Was Part Of Shuffletown

I never minded the noise from the drag strip; I just expected to hear it after church on Sunday. I used to go down there on dates, sit on top of the hood, watch the races and have a big old time. It was a social event and I got to know some of the people. Some of them I got to know good when I took over the store. They had some fancy funny cars come from all over to race at Shuffletown. I think the place was pretty famous among drag racers. Cousin Barry raced down there all the time. I had a petition to keep it open when the city was closing it because of the noise ordinance and I bet 300 or more people signed it.

Abby Rozzelle

Cotton's Threat

Cotton said that if we let one more animal in that house, we were moving to the city.

Teeny Henderson

Snakes are Drawn To The Henderson Household

When Cotton and Teeny lived in their house between Aunt Anne and Aunt Kacky's houses, somebody was always leaving the back door open and letting wild snakes in the house. Snakes just seemed to be drawn to the Henderson family. Teeny developed a good case of paranoia and a nervous tic. The kids thought it was entertaining and Cotton screamed a lot and walked around with a bat in his hands. It wasn't long after Yvonne died that they moved into Yvonne's house beside Aunt Mutt and Uncle Harrison.

Judy Rozzelle

The Bird Had A Heart Attack

One morning we got up and there was a hysterical crow flying up and down the stairs and around the ceiling. I guess the cat brought it inside. I took all the kids in the bathroom and we were all screaming. Cotton came out of the bedroom with white shaving cream on his face, wearing boxers, carrying his bat and hollering, "Where is the !@#$%^&* snake?"

About that time, the bird flew at him. "!@#$%^&," Cotton screamed. He dropped down to a crouch and was running around the den and kitchen, screaming and hollering and waving the bat at the already upset bird. In the midst of all the screaming and cursing, the bird just suddenly fell on the kitchen floor. I think it had a heart attack.

Teeny Henderson

Aunt Mabe On Mowing

Where I come from, if something needs doing you get out there and do it. When my yard needs mowing, I get on my yellow Cub Cadet riding mower and do it. I'm not so old I can't mow my own grass. I don't have time to get old.

I am very practical about mowing. I wait until late afternoon, and I dress for the occasion. I wear Bermuda shorts, a sleeveless blouse with a v-neck so I can get a little sun. Sweat does cause me to shine a little bit, and it's downright aggravating. I stuff a bunch of Kleenexes between my bosoms. Women have been doing that ever since they invented brassieres.

And to protect my hairdo, I wear a fancy blue hairnet over my curls. I start up the mower, I sit up straight, I maintain my focus to make sure I don't run over any of my chickens that sometimes follow me, and I mow in straight lines until it is done.

Mabe Jones Rozzelle

Mom's Mowing Habit

Mom was hardheaded. When I started running the store, I kept telling her not to mow the yard and I would do it, but she liked to put on her mowing garb, rev up her yellow Cub Cadet and mow. I'd just let her do it. Mom had been mowing the two or more acres of our backyard for so long people expected to see her.

Her mowing getup was a doozy. The basic outfit was a pair of Bermuda shorts and a v-necked sleeveless blouse. Being practical about the whole idea of sweating, she stuffed a wad of Kleenexes in her cleavage and to protect her weekly beauty parlor hairdo, she wore a fancy azure blue hairnet.

Then she rode up and down the backyard for hours with her back straight as a pin, wind blowing through her fancy blue hairnet and sweat rolling down into the wad of Kleenexes. I figured what the heck, let her do it, she is happy.

I always knew she was mowing when I was asked the first question about the shower cap. It took up half my morning explaining that it was her fancy blue hairnet, not a shower cap she was wearing.

Mom also kept chickens that ran free and nested in her bushes. Mom also had a green thumb and she grew everything. If she didn't plant it, she stuck it in a pot around the house. The yard right around the house was an untamed maze of growth, and anyone with good sense wouldn't go poking around looking for eggs, but Mom was out there every morning sticking her hands inside thick bushes and pulling out eggs.

Our house was in the left-hand corner of the crossroads and when they found their way out of the bushes, the chickens would peck on the side of the road for little rocks for their gizzards. And chickens do cross the road. You could sit in the kitchen anytime and hear screeching brakes and profanity.

When the first development was built near Shuffletown, the chickens made the commuters who were hurrying home so they could hurry somewhere else nervous. Every now and then someone would stop in the store and ask Dad who owned the chickens.

"They belong to Mabe," Dad would answer.

"What if I hit one of them?" they'd ask.

"You won't," he'd reply, "those chickens have been dodging cars longer than you've been driving. And if you do, we'll eat it."

We did not eat those chickens. Mama buried them.

After Dad died, Mom got particular about her pets. They had to be white. She ordered some fancy feathered white chickens. The chickens were so nervous that she had a big cage built for them. She said they were high strung. I told her they were scared of her yardful of white cats and all the people blowing their horns at them. Several customers said, "Those chickens and cats are an improvement over Sam, that mean German shepherd your Dad kept."

I told them Sam was not that mean. You just were not supposed to let him sneak up on you. But they did not believe me about this anymore than they believed Mom wore a fancy blue hairnet for mowing, and I did not have time to fool with them. One newcomer said that their yard looked like the entrance to another dimension.

Abby Rozzelle

A New Resident Adjusts

We were among the first families to move to North Woods, a new housing development near Shuffletown. My wife grew up near Lincolnton, so country living was nothing new to her, but Shuffletown was more oddly picturesque than we expected. I never understood a lot of what I saw, but on my daily drive to and from work in Charlotte, I began to watch for certain people.

For instance, once or twice a week, depending on the rainfall, when I turned left onto Mt. Holly Huntersville Road, I knew to look for an older woman mowing grass and wearing a shower cap. Her back was always rod straight and she would ride up and down for hours mowing a couple acres of grass. I just couldn't figure out why she was wearing a shower cap. Sure, she had on shorts and a blouse, but imagine how hot she must have been riding around in the sun with a shower cap on her head. And no matter how many times I saw her it distracted me and I almost ran over one of those damn chickens in the road.

Dan Phillips

Mt. Island Shopping Center

Cousin Yvonne and I extended our Sunday afternoon walks to include this new, bare dirt roadbed that ran behind Shuffletown Dragstrip and in front of the Mt. Island Shopping Center under construction.

One Sunday we came upon a skinned animal and ran all the way back to her house to call Cotton.

"Come quickly," Yvonne screamed into the telephone. "There are devil worshippers in Shuffletown. We just found a skull of a skinned animal."

"Good Grief, it is deer season," Cotton replied. "Some fool was out there stunning deer with the lights on the top of his pickup truck. They killed one and skinned it right there. I am watching NASCAR and I'll come up later."

This must have satisfied us because we walked back down to the road, although in another direction.

Bulldozers pushed down the trees, filled in the fields, drove chemically treated poles into the ground, strung electric lines and poured concrete to build Mt. Island Shopping Center. It was convenient. The grocery store managers brought samples of deli food to congregational meetings at church and gave a program on the conveniences of progress.

The road opened to traffic in 1988. When the road was finished, it was christened Brookshire Boulevard. A traffic light was hung at the intersection of Mt. Holly Huntersville Road and Brookshire Boulevard. Conveniently; it would provide easy access to Mt. Island Shopping Center. Progress? No, it is only change.

Judy Rozzelle

William Alexander (Pop-Pop) Rozzelle, Jr.

My dad, William Rozzelle, was lean, tall, and handsome for all of his eighty years. He took off his hat when he entered a home and walked with dignity. Always handy was his sly grin and his honest demeanor. He kept a book of prayers in his pocket, but kept that fact to himself. He lived an honest and respectful life and that was how he reflected his religious beliefs.

Dad had to drop out of school during the Depression to help support his family. He worked for forty-one years at the *Charlotte News* in the Circulation Department. He wore a coat and tie each day and supervised routes in the western part of the state.

The grandkids called him Pop-Pop and he was loved, but there were times that he did things that didn't compute. The best example of this was his fascination with black electrical tape. This was in a time before duct tape; Dad would have ruled the world if he had only had duct tape. He thought black electrician's tape was the answer to all repair problems from light switches to baseball gloves, saddles, books and plows.

99

Once he even tried to repair a porch swing with black tape. In theory it worked; the chain was secure until my date sat down on the swing. He dropped two feet. Dad helped him to his feet and apologized for not using enough tape.

Other things about Dad were unexplainable and best left alone. When I moved back to Shuffletown in the 80s, most every day I walked to the pond in the pasture with my dogs and cats following behind me. It was not uncommon for me to see a snake. I would always tell Dad and he would say would, "O.K. I'll go get it in a couple of days."

Sure enough, in a couple of days, Dad would say, "I took the hoe to the pond and killed the snake." How did he do that? Did the snake just stretch out his neck and surrender when Dad appeared with a hoe?

The summer he retired, he took a notion there were too many turtles in the pond. He decided to stand on the shore and shoot them. When that didn't work out as well as he planned, he bought a net and decided to row the fishing boat out into the pond. His plan was to sit very still until the turtles popped their little heads up in the waters, then he would scoop them out of the water and into the boat.

Only God and the turtles know how many times he fell in the pond, before he decided there weren't that many turtles after all. However, he repaired his net with black tape, hung it up in the barn and focused his attention on other things around the pond, leaving the pond's ecosystem intact. Like the mark of Zorro, anywhere we saw black tape we knew Dad had been there.

Anne Rozzelle Griffin

IRS Audits Good Used Cars

In 1972, the Internal Revenue Service notified Lee Wallace his business, Good Used Autos, was to be audited.

It has been a requirement for decades in Shuffletown for all young men to purchase their first clunker from Lee. This act served a purpose. The car was usually so bad off, it made us appreciate a good car when we could afford it. Lee's business headquarters is a two-room trailer built sometime in the early 50s. Lee had the trailer hauled to his car lot. In this lot, grass grows up between the used cars. In truth, Good Used Autos looks more like a junkyard than a car dealership.

Lee Wallace keeps meticulous records of each car he has ever sold. Well, at least Lee has every receipt for each car he sold in the past five decades. The receipts are all stacked in the backroom on an old sagging metal table.

On the fateful day, the IRS man dressed in an ominous dark blue suit arrives at 9:00 a.m. Lee swings the trailer door open and greets him as if he is a customer set to purchase a fleet of cars.

The IRS agent set down his briefcase, answered Lee's concerns about driving in Charlotte's morning traffic, then turned to Lee and said, "Mr. Wallace, I would like to see your receipts for a blue Mustang you sold in 1969 to a Mr. Thomas."

Lee answers, "Sure." He excuses himself and is gone for thirty long minutes, but he finally emerges from the back room of the trailer holding a receipt. Lee smiles and hands it to the blue suit.

It took until 10:30 A.M. to retrieve one more yellowed receipt. The agent asks to join Lee in the back room. It was not long before the IRS man took to coughing into a white handkerchief while watching Lee search through the stack for each receipt. By noon, the agent assures Lee that everything seems in order, shakes Lee's hand and leaves.

"Sure you don't want to buy a car while you're here?" Lee asked.

Rob Griffin

Catfish Jumps

Folks in Shuffletown have been talking about the new road since the fifties. We have always known that eventually the state would build a road that would open up Shuffletown to the galaxy. Well, it happened back in the last century, 1990, to be exact. The state began to cut a four-lane highway straight out from Charlotte. They cut down pine, oak, kudzu and sumac, pushing aside volcanic rock, pastures and cornfields. They named this road Brookshire Boulevard after a Charlotte mayor who was probably a good guy, but he had nothing to do with Shuffletown. I would bet that the city slicker who named the road did not even know a Shuffletonian.

Well, what are you going to do? Cutting the roadbed for this fancy highway meant they had to cut the Shuffletown Boat-Landing Road in half. Bulldozers pushed through the road making big mounds of asphalt and dirt on each side where it had cut the road in half. This made the Boat-Landing road as useless as a dead battery. Except the road construction did give Gus "Catfish" Davison the opportunity to act like a stunt driver for the *Dukes of Hazzard* television show. The first Sunday after they cut through the Boat-Landing Road, we heard Catfish start up his old '69 rust-red Chevy. The car was covered in rust. Cotton saw Gus drive the car slowly down Tema Circle, the road

101

in front of our house, and he saw Catfish turn left onto the old boat-landing road.

"Gus is up to something," he hollered. Gus is a little unpredictable and he's good for a laugh. He's a good old boy. I like him, but we all rushed out there to see what he was up to.

Now we had a good view of the Boat-Landing Road at that time 'cause they had cut down all the trees in our pasture and we could see straight across. This was before I planted the pine trees.

Sure enough, we could hear his car sitting on the boat-landing road. He was gunning the motor, *barroom, barroom, barroom.* That engine was wound up as tight as a hen's hiney. He was up to something. Teeny, Cotton Jr. and Jessie came out and joined us.

"What in the world is he doing?" Teeny asked.

"I think he's about to kill himself," I answered. "I think he's gonna jump the car."

Before Teeny could answer, Catfish floored the gas pedal and that rusty car flew over the mound of dirt where the Boat-Landing Road had been cut in half.

The car went airborne. We could see the rusty underbelly of the car sailing through the air; then it fell hard, like a boulder falling off a mountain; bolts flew out, doors fell off, pipes bounced and a tire rolled into the woods.

It was real quiet for a little while, and I was wondering if I needed to go in and call the fire department. Gus finally got out, walked around the car, kicked it a couple of times and got the tire out of the woods. Wasn't long before he had the tire back on the car, then he threw a couple of pipes into the car. He drove it down the new roadbed, turned it around and headed home across my pasture.

It was a funny sight. Tires were wobbling, doors were hanging off, pipes dragging on the ground, and a fender was flapping, but behind the wheel, Catfish was grinning like he had just shot a stunt scene for a movie. He did this every Sunday afternoon at three o'clock the whole summer; you could set your watch by him.

It got to where we waited to hear Catfish start his engine for another run for glory, I would grab a beer, the kids would get their sodas, Teeny would grab the chips and we headed for the back porch patio. We were settled in our chairs when the car shot into the air. It was good family entertainment.

Cotton Henderson

Shuffletown Posse

I had a bunch of break-ins at the old homeplace in the last years I lived there. Security motion alarms were installed on the screened porch, windows and doors. I did not want anyone getting in my house anymore. Five break-ins in a home were enough for a lifetime.

Unfortunately, the wind and other mythical creatures often set off the alarms. I received many of those heart-stopping calls at work from the security people saying my alarm had been set off and they were calling the police. It cost fifty dollars every time the police came out if the alarm was false. But on this day, there was nothing I could do. I had not driven my car to work. I called Aunt Mutt to see if Harry was home. He wasn't, but 79-year-old Aunt Mutt rose to the occasion.

Without telling me, she jumped into her car and drove to my house, where she jotted down the license plate of the white truck in my driveway and parked across the road to wait and see who came out of the house.

In the meantime, I called Shuffletown Grocery and told Cousin Abby what was going on. Cotton was standing there so she told Cotton to go check on it. Cotton picked up two employees at the body shop. They all grabbed a shovel or a baseball bat before they headed to my house. They had the truck surrounded when the police arrived. The police got out and walked to the front porch, banged on the door and before the police could say anything, the homeplace posse hollered,

"The posse is here. Come out now!" Hesitantly, Will Rozzelle opened the door. He had been inside checking the kitchen overhead light.

My brother, Will, confuses me. He has a doctorate in education and a master electrician's license, but he can't get the concept of how to operate a security system and when to answer a ringing phone.

The fines are costing me money, but the entertainment is worth it. Due to progress and all that crap, my kinfolks will be absorbed into the world's gene pool where all our eccentricities will be lost, diluted into the universal gene pool. We will forget what Rozzelle knees looked like, and that Pop-Pop could fix most anything with black electrical tape. Nobody fears lightning today like Aunt Kacky did. We'll forget that, except for church services, a Rozzelle could never sit in one place for longer than 20 minutes before they decided it was time to move on. We might also forget that on a March Monday a 79-year old aunt and a handful of cousins whipped together a posse in three minutes flat.

Judy Rozzelle

Baloney Burgers

Well, the truth is, my brother was the first one to serve baloney burgers. That was when he was running the place and it was known as Coy's Drive In. We had curb service back then. There was curb service at Shuffletown Grill until the late 70s. I was working part-time for Tad at Shuffletown Grocery just across the road, helping him out with whatever he needed. Tad and I seined for minnows most mornings, then I went over to cook for Coy 'round lunchtime.

One day, when he wrote the blue plate special on the board, Coy added baloney burgers to the day's menu. He taught me how to cook them and we've been serving them ever since. That's all some folks come in for. Baloney burgers got real popular after we got newspaper coverage during the Shuffletown Mayday Mayday Festival, but regular customers always liked them.

I just kept it up when he left and ran the grill for another fourteen years. At that time I got my baloney from Dellinger's Superette. You have to have good baloney. I still buy baloney in long rolls. I buy ten to fifteen pounds a week. You slice it thick for baloney burgers, 'bout 3/8 of an inch thick and I fry it on the grill. Some people like their baloney burned. You need to know how a customer prefers his baloney, but mostly you serve it with chili, slaw, mustard and ketchup. We have an "All The Way" mix that I put on my baloney. It is a mix of slaw, mustard, ketchup and onion. You let it sit and marinate. That stuff never goes bad. The longer it sits the better it is. Coy had also put this recipe together in those early days. There are a few secret ingredients I'll keep in the family. I have never run a place without putting baloney on the menu.

Leo Smith

Evening Tide

Do you ever notice twilight, the gloaming of the day? Dusk. Evening tide, when time is suspended somewhere between day and night, and shadows nip at the heels of the day. It happens every day. The blue sky turns dusty rose, streaks with orange sherbet and wisteria purple just before the light of day slides into evening shadows.

Once it was an old country tradition to sit a spell at twilight. This is when children watched for fairies on the clover and adults paused to enjoy the wonder of the beauty at the end of day.

In the time of the long before, twilight was when the oxen became restless and our ancestors prepared for the unknown lurking in the darkness of night. It was the hour to carry peat to the hearth fires, set out the meal and lead the oxen to shelter. Twilight is the gathering time.

Twilight is an opportunity to connect with the quiet of the land. Twilight visiting is not a time to speak of anything important or memorable. It is a way of being; I learned this at a very young age.

It was the only time I can recall that Momma would sit down with an empty lap. She would wipe her hands on her apron, step outside the screen door and sit with me on the top step and wait with me for the day to cool down. Most afternoons, we were also waiting for Dad to come home from work.

Sometimes, we would watch Will milk the cows by the barn. Dusk always signaled to the guinea hens it was time to gather. One by one, they would fly up to the top branches of the oak tree in the back yard and nestle in for the night.

Mom and I often would sit leaning on folded knees on the rock hard cement steps leading to the back porch. There were six wide cement steps and the cement was mixed with sledgehammered rocks. From the top cement step, you could see most all the plowed fields, the chicken house, the ripples on the pond and the orange trumpet vines growing over the pasture fence posts. Honeysuckle grew over the gate by the garden fence and at twilight, the air was feathered with sweetness.

In springtime, the yellow jonquils lined the banks of the pond. In summer, someone was always sitting with a fishing pole on the banks watching a line dangling in the water.

The cornstalks would sometime sway in the breeze and sometimes one last cow was munching on sweet grass waiting for Jimmy to lead her home.

In fall, the trees surrounding the pond were a patchwork of orange, pink, crimson and amber. The old sycamore tree was the first to turn golden and the persimmon tree hung heavy with ripe orange persimmons. As the other trees changed into their fall tresses, a colorful quilt graced the pasture and comforted the cooling waters of the pond. These brief fleeting hours bound me to the land and to family.

Like all families, the children eventually moved away. Sometimes, far away, but we always returned to gather at our parents' farm in Shuffletown. We returned to cluster for a while in our small crossroads community made up of relatives and families who had been neighbors for generations. Unnoticed, we remained this way until the scourge of city limits reached us. Now ponderous steady progress has split apart the nucleus of Shuffletown. The old cement steps, the house, the barn and even the pond have disappeared.

I did not move too far away, just a couple miles down the road. But my cousins, once as prevalent as robins, have disappeared to other places and other ways. Still, the gloaming stirs an urge in me to find someone familiar to sit with at twilight.

For too many years, I was too busy rushing home to notice twilight. But as I have become older, quieter and more appreciative of each day, sundown calls me back to old ways.

I get in my car. Call for my small dogs to jump into the front seat and drive back towards Shuffletown. Like a snapping turtle seeking water, I am drawn to Cousin Abby's backyard. Her backyard is set in a wooded grove two mailboxes past the red light at Shuffletown crossroads.

It is not necessary to call before I arrive. It is also not necessary for Abby to clean up for my visit. Family is never considered company.

When progress threatened, Abby moved from her parents' house in the corner of the crossroads by Shuffletown Grocery and bought a ranch house in a hollow not a half-mile away. She also moved everything else that had accumulated at Aunt Mabe's house in the twentieth century. This lode of forgotten treasures will yield many wonders in decades to come. It would not surprise anyone if an original copy of the Mecklenburg Declaration of Independence was found tucked among the assorted boxes. Abby even moved the craftsman-built house away from harm to a spot where it waits in safety for a new beginning.

Abby also packed up and moved the orange webbed plastic chairs Aunt Mabe bought in Florida in 1964, Uncle Ed's tool shed, several dozen or so assorted clay flower pots, a stack of buckets, a rusty glider, and three warped picnic tables built of green oak. One table was not only warped but had a broken bench. The picnic tables are good perches for her cats and kittens.

To complete the move, Abby moved her mother's plants. She dug up every plant in Aunt Mabe's yard and moved them down to her new yard in the hollow. The total count of plants transferred included approximately twenty Rose of Sharon bushes, twelve rose bushes, thirty-six day lilies, fifty-odd lamb's ear plants, assorted periwinkle and begonia plants, several dozen irises, three peony bushes, four pairs of acuba bushes, five money bushes, seven bushes no one could identify, and, to Abby's dismay, two healthy stands of poison ivy. Abby has successfully recreated the back yard of her youth.

I can never nail down an exact number of cats and kittens that live at Abby's. But there is always more than a baker's dozen and less than thirty playing in the back yard. Abby was sitting in one of the orange lawn chairs when I arrived. I noticed two of the orange webbings hung on the ground beneath her chair. The chair also was listing to one side in the uneven yard. I chose another orange lawn chair with only one strap hanging on the ground beneath it.

I settled in to share with Abby the awe of twilight and the joy of watching kittens play. They hid and explored among the flowers and the clay pots scattered about the yard.

Abby was wearing a faded housecoat and well-worn slippers. I was dressed in the usual attire, tee shirt and shorts. I quickly slipped out of my moccasins and wiggled my toes through the grass. Native Shuffletonians understand and appreciate the essence of comfortable casual attire.

Tucked away in a disheveled yard by a rutted dirt road we were bound to this moment among dappled shadows and fading sunlight. We were far away from the warp speed world.

We laugh at the cats hissing at my dogs, and anoint the newest kittens with appropriate names. We are all content, kittens, cats, dogs, and plants just there in the here and now.

The mama cat, having threatened my three small dogs sufficiently, was keeping a lazy watch on her litter. Suddenly, a kitten turns over a flowerpot; scares itself silly and in mass hysteria all kittens run for their lives to the safety of the bearded irises. Soon, a very brave kitten scuttles from beneath the foliage, arching its spine, and dances sideways like a crab stalking the menacing flowerpot. The others watch intensely, as do Abby and I. But shortly, we all lose interest and move on to other things. My dogs have lost all interest in the cats and kittens and snooze in the soft grass. And it is quiet.

We have sat like this before and we are comfortable in a way that comes only from years of sharing the same space, the same family, and the same way of life. On Sunday afternoons, our parents gathered on Grandma's front porch. The children played games such as "Are there any bears out tonight?" The bravest of the cousins was the last to join the adults on the porch as night fell like a curtain across the yard. Abby is one of the few left that I can visit with like this and wander home as contented as a cat that has just had her stomach scratched. Sitting together, we accomplish nothing specific, but in that hour, we set everything right in our world and renew for the morrow.

Life moves on and all too soon, the sun drops beneath the land and in the last light of day, we sigh to awaken our souls, gather up our shoes. Abby has a kitchen to clean and chores are waiting for me at home. Abby walks towards the back door and I open the door for the dogs to jump inside the car. The red light at Shuffletown crossroads is always green.

And when we come together on that first Sunday
the bresh arbor was as holy as any church where
God's people ever met. The cross was wound with
flowers from ever woman's garden.
We could hear the gurgle of the Long Creek. We
lifted our voices in song. Even the little birds
and crickets joined in with us...

Sunday

Sunday Was Once A Day Of Rest

Sunday was once a day when time seeped away. It was the seventh day and the day to rest. It was a day when souls condemned by original sin came together to recite in unison the *Apostles' Creed* and the *Lord's Prayer* in an effort to prepare us for the upcoming week. Sunday was the Lord's Day and the day to visit with relatives. It was a touchstone type of day.

No unnecessary chores were done on Sunday. No one finished sewing a dress on this day or plowed a field. Lawn mowers, washing machines, clothespins and tractors waited for Monday, dreaded Monday, blue Monday. On Sunday the rooster crowed twice, not once before Mom's feet touched the floor to plug in the coffee pot and to put the roast in the oven.

Time moved slowly when activities were limited to church and visiting grandparents. My mother's sisters and brothers brought their families to Poppa Sands' house in Lincolnton and they could visit for hours while cousins played together.

The men would walk out towards the pasture to talk about things men talk about. The women compared pound cake recipes and needlepoint. We knew all of our relatives, including first, second and third cousins once removed.

Sometimes after church, a family would pile in the car and set off on an aimless drive. This was referred to as "riding off somewhere." Mom and Dad liked to watch sunsets together on Sundays.

We finished up on Sunday afternoon with a visit to Grandma's house, where Dad's family gathered. Parents were older then or at least they seemed that way, and grandparents were ancient.

Grandma wore black dresses with lace collars and monstrous hats adorned with flowers and sometimes birds. Grandfathers wore suspenders and loose slacks. Poppa's Sunday-go-to-meeting shirts were starched and stiff like papier-mâché. You could hide the choir behind some of the hats women once wore.

Sunday comics were big and bright and Brenda Starr was the only woman you knew who worked outside the home. You could go all day on Sunday and nothing was expected of you, except Monday's homework.

Judy Rozzelle

The Brush Arbor

The dream of a church in Shuffletown began when the farmers and families met to worship in their homes. They shared a circuit minister with Paw Creek Presbyterian Church. The minister preached a morning service in Paw Creek and came to Shuffletown on horseback for the 2:00 p.m. services.

In the spring of 1887, the families decided to worship on the land by the curve in Rozzelle Ferry Road just north of the crossroads towards Charlotte. I believe the land belonged to a Gillis family.

The men built an arbor with tree limbs to mark their worship place, each Sunday it was decorated with hand picked flowers. It was referred to as the Brush Arbor. The Arbor was hung above the benches made from logs. They worship among nature. Honeysuckle grew in the Worship Arbor and birds built nests among the plaited limbs. While they sang hymns and prayed, mockingbirds and bluebirds sang along with them.

A clapboard house still stands near this spot of land; it is just a stone's throw from where the Fells' home place once stood. If you are coming from Charlotte on Rozzelle Ferry Road, the area is on the right and on a hill just after you cross the bridge across Long Creek.

The good folks around Shuffletown came to worship in wagons, on horseback and by foot. Some carried their shoes and crossed Long Creek in bare feet. Some snagged their best clothes in the cotton fields. Still they came faithfully each Sunday.

Gail E. Haley

A Chapel Is Built

In 1923, the small chapel in the arbor by Rozzelles Ferry Road was outgrown. Franklin Gillis donated the land beside the schoolhouse and the farmers of Shuffletown built a church.

This church would have a steeple, two Sunday school rooms that were closed off at the back by doors with frosted windowpanes, and a fan-shaped room with a center set of pews and a set on each side. There was a vestibule where the bell would be rung. Behind the church would be the graveyard.

110

Sloan's Memorial Presbyterian Church came to be upon this ground. Sunday school began at 2 pm and preaching at 3 pm. To have lights in the church, they laid a large tank in the ground, partially filled with water, and a hopper filled with carbide granules. There was a bell sealed inside the tank. When the carbide granules burst creating gas, the gas created pressure that made the bell rise up through the pipes and turned on the church lights.

One dark evening, Harrison Rozzelle and Tom Gillis went out to check the pressure on the bell. The sun had just dropped over the edge of the horizon and the yard was dark. They couldn't see the bell, so someone struck a match. The next time Harrison and Tom were seen, each one had bandages on their hands.

Another time, Scott Cameron was standing by when someone was looking at the bell. They jokingly suggested that they ought to strike a match. "I'm scared to even let moonlight shine in there," Mr. Scott replied.

In late July or August, local churches held picnics and baseball games. This was "the laying by time" when the crops have grown taller than the weeds could catch up. It is when the season's planting and plowing are done, and the crops are left to grow.

The picnics were all day affairs. There was always an acre of tablecloths laid end to end and covered with fried chicken, deviled eggs, string beans, potato salad, biscuits, cakes and pies from every kitchen in the community. Lemonade was made in big washtubs and everyone bought a dipper full.

The church baseball teams challenged the mill teams. When the first ball was pitched, farmers became the 'boys of summer.' Everyone felt younger on this day.

The children played Rover, Red Rover Come on Over, Ring around the Posey and Drop the Handkerchief. The teenagers played Snap. When they weren't playing Snap, the boys pretended not to notice the girls and the girls tried not to giggle.

The ice truck would come from Mt. Holly, bring the ice and bury it in sawdust. It was a special treat when a child was allowed to chip off the corner of a block of ice and eat it. Everyone would bring his or her own milk, sugar, and freezer to make ice cream and sell it for a nickel to make money for the church.

Each boy took his turn cranking the ice cream churn and each was rewarded with a free cup of the best ice cream ever made. In the evening, there was singing on the grounds.

Revivals were held during these times. There was preaching on the grounds every night for a week. Babies were baptized, people joined the church and some were married.

When the harvest was ready and the sun was high in the summer sky, the families would meet at a neighbor's farm and shuck corn half the night or until they served cakes and pies. Families raised most of what they needed, but they could trade or carry a debt at the general store until harvest time. This was usually the total of a family's debt for a lifetime.

At harvest time, someone with a threshing machine would come around to the farms and thresh the wheat. The threshers would spend the night on the farm. The next morning a hearty breakfast of homemade sausage, eggs, bacon and biscuits was served. Farmers always prayed for good weather during the threshers' visit. If it rained, they were responsible for feeding the men until they could get back to their threshing. Several days of rain could hurt the family's economy in a bad way.

Wallace Innis

Sunday Morning At Cousin Kissey's

It was a long time ago, but I still remember going to the big house on Sunday morning to see Grandma Anne and Cousin Kissey. They always had a treat for us. Grandma Anne was born and grew up in the big house and she was really my aunt. She and Cousin Kissey worked awfully hard running the place. The other children, Kacky, William and Tad, were mostly grown when Johnny and I came along. When my Dad finished his chores, he would lift us up to the buggy seats and ride off to the big house. He would lift us down and we ran up the steps and across the porch. We knew our treat was waiting.

The front porch wrapped around the side of the house and connected with the middle porch that separated the dining room and the kitchen from the main part of the house. I am sure that sometimes we stayed inside the house. We went every Sunday and in the wintertime, but when I remember those days, it seems it was always summer. We sat on the middle porch and we didn't stay long. Mama was home fixing dinner and we had to be at church by two in the afternoon. Our church shared a preacher with Paw Creek Methodist and he preached at our church in the afternoon.

Cousin Kissey did not make us wait, our treat was always ready and she brought it out to the porch immediately. It was always the same, little custard pies. They were made with sweet cream, eggs and sugar. We could have only one. We knew not to even ask for another, but it was gone in three bites. It was like eating soft velvet and it was tart. The custard left your mouth puckered and craving. My goodness, I always wanted just one more, but Cousin Kissey had made them for the folks coming to the Johnson House for dinner.

The porches were filled with rocking chairs. Everyone who came for dinner would have a chance to sit and rock. Think of all the people who came to eat and afterwards sat down to rock back and forth to watch the river roll past them. Like they didn't have a care in the world and they had everything to care about. I still recall that slow way of rocking and the creak of the rockers on the wood floor.

I never knew my grandparents, Vernon and Smiley Johnson. I wish I had. I like to think that Grandma Smiley would have given us another custard.

Anne Rozzelle McCall

Pearl Harbor

Pearl Harbor happened on a Sunday. I was with a bunch of boys hanging out at a gas station on Statesville Road. Someone had a car radio on and suddenly they stopped our world by announcing the bombing of our ships. I enlisted in the Navy on Monday.

Wallace Innis

Gail Played The Marimba

There were no stages or talent scouts in Shuffletown; the only entertainment in Shuffletown revolved around church activities and the occasional piano or dance recital. A trip to Hollywood, the home of the silver screen, would require more than a day's drive and money. These stark facts raised Louise Einhart's role as a frustrated stage mother to an art form.

In desperation, ever so often Louise would volunteer her daughter, Gail, to play the marimba for the congregation during Sunday preaching. It was quite a treat. Until Gail played, no one in the whole congregation had ever seen a marimba, much less heard one played.

Our musical knowledge was attained mostly from the *Ed Sullivan Show*. Louise always scheduled Gail to play for national holidays and high holy days occasions at the church.

Gail would stand in front of the church holding in each hand a stick with a rubber ball at the end. With the sticks, she would hit the brass and wood contraption, creating music. We probably paid her more attention than the preacher on those Sundays. The feat looked harder than two-tree plowing with a stubborn mule. I have little idea of what that is either, but I truly recall watching both plowing and Gail's performances in awe.

I rank both tasks in the category of futile, laborious, hard-won and beyond the ability of most mortals. They are Herculean tasks like golf, competitive ice-skating and folding contoured sheets.

Now fifty years later, Gail Einhart Haley has published 35 children's books. She has won the Caldecott Medal and the Kate Greenway Award for excellence in children's literature. But in Shuffletown, everyone over fifty remembers the girl who played the marimba in church. Eventually, in every conversation with a Shuffletonian, she knows they will realize exactly whose daughter she is and will ask, "Aren't you the girl who played the marimba in church?" The younger set inquires, "Are you the girl my mother told me about who played the marimba in church?"

Judy Rozzelle

Harry Lifts Weights

Sister Yvonne was a tiny skinny thing, even when she was all grown up. But when she got mad it was like having a mean little chicken after you.

One Sunday morning when Mom and Dad were at the beach, I went outside to lift weights. It was my morning routine. I'd been doing it awhile and I could press a lot of weight, over two hundred pounds. Don't know what happened that morning but after I got 'em up there, when I was bringing them down I lost my balance and fell backwards.

The weights landed across my neck and pinned me to the ground. Didn't hurt myself, but I couldn't move. So, I hollered for Yvonne, who had moved back home with us after her second divorce. I knew she was sitting at the kitchen table, drinking coffee and reading the paper. She did not answer but I kept hollering for her.

Finally she opened the back door, stomped down the steps in her bright orange velour robe and stood there looking down at me.

"What damn fool thing have you done now?" she said. "Why don't you get up?"

Well, I could not get up, or I would not have called her.

"Could you help get this thing off of me?"

"You idiot, I can't lift that thing."

If I could have stood up, I would have hit her. "Just lift one side and let's see if we can lift it together," I asked. So, she bent down and gave it a little pull. I could not get a good grip at that angle and about all I could do was grunt and push at it. We kept trying and all the while, we were hollering at each other. Finally, we did get the weight off the ground, but then Yvonne dropped it on my Adam's apple. God, that hurt, and I told her so. She cussed me back, and she could cuss better'n any sailor I ever met. They could have heard us at church.

"That's it," she said after about ten minutes of insults. "I'm going in and calling Sloan's VFD. Then I'm going to finish my coffee." She started stomping towards the house.

"You call them and I'll kill you in your sleep," I hollered after her. I heard the door slam. Teeny, my niece, was about seven and she came out to stand over me and laugh.

That did it. I lifted one side off me, ran inside and yanked the phone away from Yvonne. I fixed my bicycle tires and rode off on it before the folks got home from church. I never messed with weights again.

Harry Rozzelle

Harry Cleans His Gun

One Sunday Uncle Harry was cleaning his gun and he blew a hole in his bedroom wall. Everyone was gone somewhere but Harry and me. I was watching television in the den and I heard this loud *kaboom*. I thought, "Oh God, what has Uncle Harry done?"

I ran back to his room and he was sitting on the edge of his bed, grinning his stupid sideways grin with his rifle between his legs. He had all of his guns laid out on the carpet.

He nodded for me to come in and look. That nut had blown a hole in the wall right in front of him between the chest of drawers and the closet. Smoke was still drifting out of the hole.

"Do you think Mom will notice the hole?" he asked.

The hole was as big as a golf ball, but I answered, "Naw, Harry, she won't ever notice a hole in her wall. You IDIOT."

I went back to the den and laughed my head off. When I left, he found one of those big red stickers the fire departments gave out that you were supposed to put in your kid's bedroom window in case of fire. In a little bit, he called me back to his room. He had found one of those stickers and he had put it over the bullet hole. Uncle Harry thought he had found a good solution.

"I don't think she'll notice it right away. What do you think?" he asked.

I was still laughing, but I said, "Uncle Harry, why don't you go buy a picture and hang it there?"

"She'll know I did something if I hang a picture there," he replied. Momma Mutt came home that night and took every gun Uncle Harry had and hid them. There is one pretty little silver pistol she hid so well we haven't found it to this day.

Teeny Henderson

Sunday Pranks

I never knew what Jim Bob was going to do to me next. He would pull a prank on me anywhere, even church. When I was a deacon, I'd pass the offering plate along the rows the third Sunday of every month. I did this for a couple of years.

One Sunday, ole Jim Bob must have noticed a hoppy toad on the way into church. Cause that third Sunday, when he handed me back the offering plate, he smiled and dropped the toad in the offering. I grabbed the toad and I could not stuff it in my pocket or it would have looked like I taking money from the church offering. I had to continue on down the aisle with a toad in my fist and act regular. I had to hold that darn toad during the whole sermon before I could walk outside and drop it out of my sweaty palm on the ground.

That wasn't the only Sunday he pulled a stunt. One Sunday morning the boy wasn't even planning on going to church but around eleven o'clock, he was seen driving a little too fast by a state trooper on the road in front of the church. Jim Bob saw the trooper turn around to come after him and he decided to best thing to do was to go to church. I guess Jim Bob knew the trooper saw him turn into the church parking lot. After church, Jim Bob came up with some cockamamie reason to ask me to drive his car home for him following the services. I didn't get out of the parking lot before the trooper pulled me over. Everybody leaving church saw me. The trooper did not believe a word I said, but I did convince him to follow me to Jim Bob's house to give him the ticket.

Slick Cameron

The Carnivore Keeshonds

I run from dogs every Sunday to get inside Aunt Mutt's house to eat. But Aunt Mutt's homecooked food is worth it, even if I'm wounded.

Rozzelle dogs usually match their owners in little eccentric ways. Take the two dogs that share the adjoining land around Teeny and Cotton's house and Aunt Mutt and Uncle Harrison's house. They are meat eaters.

In the past their indiscriminate diet has consisted of the leg muscles of kinfolk, neighbors, friends and a few strangers, who will never pass this way again. The most often asked question when I run into an old friend of theirs who hasn't been around in a while is, "Do they still have the big gray dog that bites? She bit me."

"Well, they do still have that dog, Lizzie. She is a keeshond who has presented Teeny with many puppies to sell, guards her kids and bites repairmen who charge by the hour," I answer.

When Cotton and Teeny moved the family into the house Yvonne built, Teeny acquired another keeshond, Samson, to guard Uncle Harrison's house.

Samson is a larger version of Lizzie, but like most males, not as active. He snarls, growls and watches for potential visitors, but Samson rarely commits to actually lunging towards you for a bite. He lets Lizzie do that. Lizzie just appears, runs straight to a leg and chomps down into the flesh. She is not a shy dog.

My modus operandi for Sunday dinner is to beep the horn until someone hears me and comes out to hold the dogs for my safe passage.

If Samson is the only dog in the yard, I bravely take four giant steps from the car to the porch, all the while talking to Samson, using words like *stay...oh...please...please stay...that's a nice dog*. The giant steps are taken between the begging and the pleading. The fear is comparable to swimming with sharks.

But today, when I pulled into Aunt Mutt's backyard for Sunday dinner (this is lunch to you newcomers), danger was stretched out and waiting. Lizzie was laid out in the middle of the driveway. She sat up to watch as my car rolled to a halt. Samson was on the top porch step, blocking my path to Aunt Mutt's pot roast. I blew the horn. No one answered. I blew the horn again to no avail. Surely one of the kids would hear, I thought, they will come out and call off the dogs. I leaned on the horn, again and again.

This is ridiculous, I thought. I am a grown woman and those damn dogs know me, which of course was part of the problem. This standoff was a continuing tactical game between me and two deranged dogs. Lizzie yawned, laid back down and Samson slept. I opened the car door and leaned outward, placing one foot on the ground. Lizzie stood up and growled. Samson began to stare at me.

Silent monitors in my brain suggested I should go home and fix a sandwich. But I was determined that nothing was going to stand between me and Aunt Mutt's fresh green beans. I got back in the car, blew the horn and waited again, but no one came to the door.

Finally, I started the engine. I had a plan. Uncle Harrison's driveway wraps around his house from the road like a horseshoe. This shape provides two driveway entrances from the highway. I was going to drive out one driveway and back in the other side with the objective of driving faster than the dogs could run and lunging myself into the house.

The moment the engine started the dogs jumped up, ran barking at my car wheels. There was a dog running and barking on each side of my car. When I stopped at the end of the driveway to look for traffic they lost interest. It was obvious to them that they had driven me off. They began sniffing and peeing in celebration.

I turned left onto the highway, drove the 50 yards to the other driveway entrance, whipped around the corner of the house at a reckless speed, parked inches from the porch steps and stepped safely inside the screen door just as the keeshonds came tearing around the back of the house. I slammed the door and hollered, "I made it."

"Well, you better get in here," Aunt Mutt answered. "What kept you?"

"Cotton had the dogs out there holding me off until he got all the food he wanted," I answered as I grabbed a plate and sat down.

"That's right," Cotton answered as he helped himself to more potatoes.

Teeny went into the kitchen to refill her tea glass. "Judy," she hollered. "Your car is still running."

Judy Rozzelle

Communion Wafers

Communion at church was an auspicious event. Even though we passed grape juice instead of wine, the communion wafers were authentic we made them ourselves. Communion services were celebrated every couple of months.

The communion wafers were made on Saturday afternoon in the kitchens of the women of the church. Usually it took two women and a whole afternoon to get the task done.

Jo Rozzelle and I were often called upon to make the wafers. We did the baking while our kids played out in the yard. We slapped and kneaded the dough, then rolled it out with a rolling pin till it was almost thin enough to see through less than an eighth of an inch thick. Then we cut the dough into wafers with a special utensil that had a crinkly edge. When the last wafer had come out of the oven, we placed them all on silver plates and covered the plates with lace.

A lot of wafers were burned on those Saturday afternoons. They were easy to burn, being so thin and fragile. We did not want any one from church eating burned sacraments. We took a lot of pride in baking perfect wafers.

Each time they came out burned, we had to start over. But we didn't throw out those blackened wafers: heavens no. We fed them to the children. We always gave them a cup of grape juice, too, to wash them down. I figure our kids consumed enough sacraments those Saturdays to thoroughly cleanse their heathen little souls.

Mutt Rozzelle

Sloan's Volunteer Fire Department
Est. 1952
Motto: We Never Lose a Foundation

Mutt Sets Off The Alarm

When the Fire Department was first organized, I worked at home like most women. They couldn't afford a radio system so they asked me if they could list me as the emergency contact and I said, "Sure, why not?"

So they tacked a big chalkboard on the front of the building. When someone called to tell me about a fire, I took the message, took off my apron and ran down the hill and across the highway, set off the siren and wrote the location down on the board. Then I ran back across the road and got out of the way.

Mutt Rozzelle

A Brand New Fire Truck

We bought our first fire truck used from the Pinoca Volunteer Fire Department. We got our first brand new cherry red fire truck in 1962. Everyone showed up for the occasion, and of course, we had to try out the hose. Fred Anderson, Dunk Cooper and me were holding the water hose when they turned on the water. I have forgotten how many gallons of water it shot out, but it was powerful.

The ground got soaked in no time. We were standing in mud trying to aim the stream of water into the woods by the Fire Department. Then someone decided to turn up the water flow and pressure. The water pressure kicked Fred and me off the hose. It felt like I had been bucked out of the saddle by a wild horse. Some others were trying to get to the hose, but they kept slipping in the mud. For a long, long time it was just Dunk Cooper and the hose. The hose almost beat him to death. It slung him all over the place. The water stream shot across the road, above the passing cars, then Dunk got it back into the woods, the water bent the little saplings backwards in the woods, broke a couple of tree limbs, and spit dirt and sticks into the air. It was chaos. Dunk was screaming

121

and no one could get to the hose. Finally, Bill Short noticed and he cut off the water. It was a while before we learned how to run the hose. But we stayed at it and by the first fire call we were ready to roll.

Slick Cameron

The Fire Siren

They test the fire siren at Sloan's VFD every Monday night at exactly eight pm. You can set your clock by it.

Jerry Goode

The Screaming Siren

That siren used to scare me to death every Monday night when it went off. I always thought, "Oh God, whose house is on fire?" I always ran to the front window and looked out to see which way the fire engines turned at the crossroads. It took a while to get used to, but now when I hear the siren on Monday night, wherever I am, I know all is well in Shuffletown.

Yvonne Rozzelle Herbert

Town Limits

There are not any real boundaries to Shuffletown. There were no signs "You are entering Shuffletown." Or any signs "You are leaving Shuffletown." I always thought it was more a state of mind. Seriously, I couldn't exactly pinpoint what made you a Shuffletonian except your state of mind. Then one night after I moved down the road to Coulwood, I was surprised to hear the Monday night eight o'clock siren. It made me feel so good that I decided that along with a state of mind the one qualifying rule of thumb was that if you could hear the fire siren you were a Shuffletonian. You know, like the citizens of London were Cockneys if they could hear the bells of St. Mary's when they rang.

Judy Rozzelle

In 1966, I Owned An Emerald Green Mustang

I was single, the car was fast, and life was good. On the weekend I hardly ever rolled into my driveway before two a.m. Sometimes it was close to dawn.

That Mustang was a beauty. I washed and waxed her weekly. If the sun was harsh or it had rained a lot, I waxed her more often. I had special order chrome hubcaps on her wheels. Friday nights some of us boys would pile in my car and cruise through drive-in restaurants. There was never an evening we didn't get several girls' telephone numbers, unless, of course, we had a date. My car was a girl magnet.

It was well past midnight one Friday night when, on my way home, I smelled something burning. I had just come across the little bridge at Long Creek. I looked over my shoulder and saw a lit cigarette in the backseat. I could see the glow because the road got black-dark after ten o'clock back then.

Well, I was less than a mile from Sloan Volunteer Fire Department. So I figured the smartest thing to do was to gun the gas, get to the station and set off the alarm. But when I got there, I couldn't figure out how to set it off. I tried to put out the smoldering seat with my jacket, but it seemed to make it worse.

I decided to run to the pay phone at the crossroads and call my friend, Dunk. Man, I hated leaving my car, but I had to do something. I ran like hell to the phone and while Dunk's phone was ringing, I saw flames spring up bright and tall in the back seat. It was an awful sight.

Dunk was groggy when he answered the phone. "DUNK!" I screamed, "I've got a FIRE in my backseat and you have got to get down here." I slammed down the phone and ran back to my car; although there wasn't a dang thing I could do but wait.

Dunk, though, wasn't thinking straight. He took time to brush his teeth, comb his hair, and make himself smell good. He put on his best pants and a freshly pressed shirt.

When he arrived and saw the flames he jumped out of his car cursing like a sailor. "Aw, HELL!" he said, "I thought you meant you had a woman in your back seat on fire."

He set off the alarm and it didn't take long for the locals to arrive in their heavy hats and uniforms. But in my terrible hurry, I had parked the Mustang right in front of the bay and they couldn't pull the fire truck out to operate the hoses. The car was so close to the door they couldn't even inch the truck forward. They did finally pull the hoses off in time to keep the fire from reaching the gas tank. But by then the car was a total ruin.

When the flames were out, we sat on the truck beds and watched the Mustang smoke. Then the ribbing began. I had just lost my car, and those boys wouldn't shut up.

Dunk drove me home. I just left my Mustang there. I don't know who pushed it behind the fire station, but it sat there for a long time until finally it got towed away. I stayed away. I couldn't stand to look at it, for one thing. But I knew they were talking about me and Dunk and how we let my Mustang burn up in front of a fire station. Hell, they still are.

Barry Smith

The Fire Chief

When Rob was Chief of the Volunteer Fire Department, he insisted on keeping the legs of his volunteer fireman uniform tucked in his boots in the corner of the bedroom ready for the next fire. To this day, I miss the police scanner he kept on in the bedroom.

Anne Griffin

The Fire Chief Faints

We are supposed to respond quickly and correctly to any medical emergencies in Shuffletown as well as fires. So we thought it'd be a good idea to review our EMT skills. We started watching training films at the regular Monday night firehouse meetings. And that is when we learned we'd better not rely on Rob Griffin in any medical emergencies.

It was the night we watched a film about car wrecks. It was pretty graphic, nothing but blood and smashed bodies, but we didn't think anything of it. When I cut on the lights, however, Rob was slumped in his chair.

We thought he'd had a heart attack. We whipped into action. Dunk and Cotton slid him out of his chair down onto the floor. We stretched him out, loosened his clothes and got into our positions. I knelt over him to administer CPR. Jerome pinched his nose, pulled his mouth open and checked his airways. We knew all about the Golden Hour — how minutes, seconds count when you are oxygen-deprived.

Jerome was about to give Rob the breath of life when suddenly Bob opened his eyes. Jerome's face was about three inches away at this point, and I was sitting on Bob.

"Just what the hell do y'all think you're DOING?" he blurted, throwing us off and jumping to his feet. "I just PASSED OUT! I always do that when I see blood! GOOD GRIEF!"

Rob stomped out, hopped in his truck, and drove off.

Who would have figured that the fire chief couldn't stand the sight of blood?

Slick Cameron

The Animal Breather

I've saved a couple of lives doing mouth-to-mouth. They haven't all been people, though.

One time we got called to put out a trailer fire. We get a lot of calls for trailer fires, but it is hard to get to them in time because those things can go up in flames in two minutes flat. Anyhow, this one was a new doublewide and we managed to get the people out in time. Only their German shepherd was so confused, he kept running in and out of the trailer. I guess he was trying to make sure everyone was out of danger. Finally, the smoke got to him and he collapsed in the yard. Heck, I was not going to let him go. I stretched him out and gave him mouth to mouth. I did the whole CPR routine, pushing on his chest and breathing in his muzzle. Wasn't too long before the dog came around and got up. He was weak but he was all right.

A week later, we got a call from the Rocking K Ranch. A horse had fallen on a girl and broken her leg. When we got there, we were shocked to find the horse still on top of the girl. He was dead. They said he was an old horse and had just keeled over.

Well, every fireman that had shown up kept hollering for me to give the horse mouth-to-mouth. In fact, every time we go out on a call the guys look for an animal for me to save. I am the animal breather.

Jerry Goode

Burning The Gaines Sisters' Century-Old Home

After Mamie and Esther Gaines died, the family asked the Fire Department to burn the old house down. That was a shame; that house was over a hundred years old. It was built with wooden nails. I went in the house several times and tried to look through their stuff before we burned it.

Those women kept everything they ever had, and they had lived a long time. I hate to think what all went up in flames with that house. I salvaged a lot of stuff, but I didn't have time to get much.

I found the old war ration books for both Miss Mamie and Miss Esther. I have them here somewhere. From 1941 until 1945 or 1946, I've forgotten when the rationing stopped, but in every one of the rationing books for all those years both of the ladies listed their ages as 48.

Rob Griffin

VFD Assists Jenny And G-G Grant

When Jenny and G-G moved into the vacant colored schoolhouse and made it their home in the 1940s, they did not add a bathroom. I didn't know this until long after I was grown. Everyone had bathrooms by this time or at least we thought they did, but Jenny and G-G were still using an outhouse. In the late 70s, they were both already retired when Beth Nixon told someone about them not having an indoor bathroom. When the members of the Sloan Volunteer Fire Station heard this news, they immediately made a project of installing a bathroom in their home. The Volunteer Fire Department did a bunch of good deeds other than putting out fires for the neighbors.

Judy Rozzelle

The Buddy System

When I was a kid, if you heard a siren around here you knew someone had drowned. People were always drowning in the Catawba River. So in the seventies, Sloan Fire Department established and trained several volunteer firemen as a search and rescue dive team on the river. It was a good idea, but they pulled out only one man alive. Mostly, the calls came in too late for us to do any good.

One Fourth of July we got a call that there was a drowning at the Shuffletown Boat Landing. Me and Dunk met at the Fire Department, got out the rescue truck, hooked up the boat, turned on the siren, and made it to the landing in record time. The crowd there waved us over towards the right where the picnic tables were. We jumped out of the truck, and ran over to the riverbank, where lots of picnickers were standing. Several of them were crying. Nobody was in the river but one man, and he was just standing out there up to his neck in water.

I turned to the bystanders. "Can anyone show us where the victim went down, so we know where to dive?" I yelled.

"I know where he is," hollered back the man in the river. "I'm standing on him."

I dived in the water to one side of him and Dunk dove in the river from the other. Sure enough, we could see white trunks shimmering in the current under the muddy water. We brought up the body and his buddy swam to shore with us.

That was some buddy system.

Barry Smith

Cotton Sets Himself On Fire

Couple times a year, I cook the pigs for the Volunteer Fire Department barbecue. Used to be an annual thing but it got so popular now we have one pretty much whenever we feel like it. I slow-roast the pigs up here at the shop, and it takes about a week to get them done just right. I do it not because I am a fireman, but because I am a good cook. I have been known to throw some deer meat, fish or whatever else I've caught fresh on the grill for us to eat while we're painting cars or fixing up the smashed ones.

I've also been known to set myself on fire.

Aw, you know how it is. Gas grills don't always work right. It's hard to tell when one is going to belch flame at you. Also, when we set up, me 'n' Gene usually end up burned a little. Teeny says we end up smoking like chimneys.

Well, last year, the first day of cooking, I set myself on fire three times. I singed my head real good, and then when I lit the second grill it caught the edge of my shirt on fire. When I lit the third, it blew Gene and me back about fifteen feet.

That was when Jerry Goode decided maybe we ought to keep one of the Fire Department's EMT trucks up here at the shop. I must have looked bad, because he went to go get it, right then and there. Me, I got in my truck and rode off to get my hair trimmed real short. I figured it was going to be a long week, getting those grills going.

Cotton Henderson

Cotton's Secret Barbeque Sauce

The following recipe makes a couple gallons of BBQ sauce for base.
1-2 handful of vinegar
1 handful onion salt
1 handful black pepper
Little bit Texas Pete
A bunch of crushed red pepper

I may have left out four or five ingredients, I'm not sure, but this will get you started. Be careful when you fire up the grill. That can be a little tricky.

Burning Duke's

Duke's Fix It Shop stood empty for several years after he passed away. His family gave the Fire Department permission to burn the place down. We brought the fire trucks down to the corner. We started the first fire around ten 'clock that morning and spent all day setting the building on fire and putting it out. When the afternoon got late, we put out the fire for the last time and started taking the trucks and the equipment back to the station.

Just to make sure there were not any live embers still hot, I stayed behind with one old fire truck. I was dirty and sweaty. My uniform was covered with soot and I was leaning on the truck studying the ashes to make sure the fire was out.

This lady pulled up in her station wagon. She leaned out the door and hollered, "I'm sorry you lost your house. If you hadn't had to fight it alone, you might have saved it."

Rob Griffin

The Shuffletown Mayday Mayday Festival And Yard Sale

ALL NEW—COMPLETELY UPDATED and Unauthorized
OFFICIAL SOUVENIR AND GUIDEBOOK TO
SHUFFLETOWN

Home of Drag Racing, Minnow Farming, and the
World-Famous Baloney Burger
Immerse yourself in the culture, food and history of Shuffletown,
a semi-scenic crossroads community just a few brick loads shy of
becoming another Blockbuster Video shopping complex
Lincoln's paternity exposed!

FEATURING:
- Unverified genealogy of Shuffletown's First Families
- Unsubstantiated first-person accounts of historic,
  memorable, or just plain odd events
- Incomplete recipes of Cotton's Barbeque Sauce and
  Mama Jo's Stickies.
- Undiscovered production of Billie Bob and Miranda,
  Shakespeare on the Catawba
- Not-too-hard instructions on how to create your own
  hometown tourist guide

Shuffletown Mayday-Mayday Festival and Yard Sale Events

<u>Keynote Speech "The Parentage of Abraham Lincoln"</u>: Based on
decades of hearsay and documented rumors, Senator John Calhoun
of South Carolina was a frequent guest at the Rozzelle Ferry Inn
and Restaurant at the same time Nancy Hanks, Honest Abe's mom,
was working at the Rozzelle Inn as a big-hearted, but misunderstood
waitress. The speech will recount the friendship that evolved between Hanks and Calhoun leaving no doubt as to the paternity of our
16th President.

The Hands-On Science Museum: Visitors will hear a lecture at Shuffletown Grocery on how to farm minnows and harvest them.

Human Race: Eligibility limited to qualified entrants.

The Catawba River Regatta: To be held the weekend before the Festival by visiting dignitaries, members of the press, and virgins over forty.

The Shuffletown Grill: Featuring the World-Famous Baloney Burger. Franchises will be made available during the Mayday Mayday Festival.

A one-time "by invitation only" showing of Da Vinci's "Lost Pieta," which was discovered among various other objets d'art in Shuffletonian yards and garages. Other yard art to be displayed includes such treasures as Froggie Teatime, Blue Madonna, Bambi, a mirrored ball, and a non-racist Footman. The evening gala would include an auction of velvet paintings, Elvis memorabilia, and other investment quality art.

A Shakespearean Drama: The Shuffletown Shakespeare Society will present a drama, written by Yvonne Herbert's High School Drama Class, to be presented in Carter's cornfield located behind Mack Gillis's Service Station.

Debutante Ball and Cotillion: To be held at Cotton's Paint and Body Shop. Invited dignitaries included: Ron Reagan, Pope John Paul, Princess Di (husband optional), Andy Warhol, Jimmy Hoffa, Dolly Parton, Elvis Pressley, and special guest, Willie Nelson, who would be invited as the festival sex symbol. Snobby celebs who do not show will be sent a certificate of Non-Participation and fined thereafter every time they are seen in Shuffletown.

Compiled from Press Releases - Spring 1983

Yvonne Introduces The Mayday Mayday Festival

From the get go, the Shuffletown Mayday Mayday Festival and Yard Sale was Cousin Judy's dang fool idea.

One evening right after Cousin moved home to Shuffletown, we were having hot tea and honey at her house to fight our colds. After a couple of cups, we started moaning about how there was so much traffic at the crossroads two of Aunt Mabe's chickens had been run over in the last month. Aunt Mabe's free-range chickens were part of our heritage, and everyone in Shuffletown knew to watch for them when they turned at the crossroads.

Now commuters were wiping out our chickens like they once did the buffalo. One thing led to another, Cousin Judy spoke of the aggravation of zip codes, nuclear fallout, and other signs of progress.

Jon Ponder, Cousin Judy's wacko business partner, joined us and after a few cups of tea, he was as enthusiastic as my village idiot relative. Before you knew it, they had decided that a semi-scenic place like Shuffletown should take its place among the tourist traps of the South, like Charleston, home of the Spoleto Festival, and Spivey's Corner, home of the Hollerin' Contest. Before I knew it, Cousin and Jon had discovered that Shuffletown is the center of a population radius that contains almost 60% of the people of the United States. That is significant compared to Atlanta's 43%, New York's 47% or Spivey's Corner's 59.3%.

Their writing was barely legible, but they were acting like they had just struck gold. Yeah, well I kept feeling like they were holding a match near dynamite. Jon said that May was only two months away and Shuffletown should have a Mayday Festival. Then Cousin said, "Oh, no…it has to be a Mayday Mayday Festival because we are sounding the alarm that progress was eating up Shuffletown."

Well, if these idiots were going to have a festival and draw people out here, I figured I may as well have a yard sale. They agreed, naturally, and the Shuffletown Mayday Mayday Festival and Yard Sale was launched.

Then they decided to draw attention to the festival by entering a float in Charlotte's St. Patrick's Day parade. Their float was going to be a broken down pick up truck with two goats painted green with cake coloring riding in the back. They started calling people and inviting them to be on the festival's publicity committee. Let me assure you, no one who received their phone calls understood what either of the idiots was talking about, but Judy said that was no problem, she would call them tomorrow and explain everything. If it had been me, I would have called them the next day and denied the whole thing. Anyhow, the madness had escaped Pandora's Box and I agreed to be co-chair of the festival because somebody needed to keep them out of trouble. Every time something like this happens, I'm obligated to keep her from making a fool out of herself and this time she included the entire of Shuffletown in her scheme. I figured they would surely end up running her out of town on this one.

Yvonne Rozzelle Herbert

Kays Gary, Columnist, The *Charlotte Observer*, May 1983

Civic-minded citizens of Mecklenburg's Shuffletown are ready to make a run at Spivey's Corner as the king of media-event bucolic culture.

Spivey's Corner, as the Western World has acknowledged, is a crossroads twenty miles east of Fayetteville that built its fame with a National Hollerin' Contest each June.

Spivey's Corner is also noted for its futile invitations to host the Super Bowl, World's Fair and Olympics.

Now comes Shuffletown, a Mecklenburg crossroads eight miles northwest of Charlotte on NC 16, joining the ranks of Spring Festival promoters, with the first "Mayday Mayday Festival and Yard Sale" Saturday and Sunday, May 7-8.

There'll be a parade unlike traditional parades.

Stationary Parade

In this one, the parade will stand still and the people will walk around it to band music. Everybody is supposed to bring transistor radios. Many events have been scheduled, most conflicting with each other, but every first-time event has problems, and we fully expect crowds ranging between fifty and ten thousand.

Judy Rozzelle

I Had Nothing To Do With It...

For the record, let me state, again, that it took several meetings to plan this festival. And I will not be held accountable for one dang fool idea that came about during these meetings other than the yard sale and the Velcro bow ties to be sold at the barn ball. During these meetings, that I deny ever attending, I also served in the responsible capacity of seeing that the esteemed idiots who also deny ever attending the meetings did not drive home drunk. However, it took me more than two hours to sober up the idiots who were not here in the first place.

Yvonne Rozzelle Herbert

Selling Heritage

Heritage is the keynote of the event. So, the yard sale is for people who want to get rid of unwanted heritage. We will have a cultural tour on Saturday and a historical tour on Sunday including a stop by Laura's Rozzelle House, site of the only Civil War battle fought in Mecklenburg County.

Judy Rozzelle

Kays Gary, Columnist, The *Charlotte Observer*, May 1983

But crowds did converge on this town that isn't and yet has been for 180 years. And what they did was tour the attic sales and talk; buy cakes at bake sales and talk; listen to the string band and talk, and walk around while the parade of antique cars, a replica of the old Rozzelles Ferry, several dogs, a horse, tractor and some pickup trucks stood still.

What we did mostly was enjoy and remember the ways some things were and few things are and celebrate this place.

One could hope small crossroads communities across America would join the likes of Shuffletown in annual celebration. They birthed, after all, a nation.

Printed with permission of the Charlotte Observer

Crossing Over

Time

Time, like a river, flows endlessly. And with its passing the footprints and echoes of those who once lived upon the land are swept away. The laughter, the tears, the joy of their lives disappears into the unknown, even to those who inherit their blood and other resemblances. Their time on earth becomes obscure dates etched in stone in quiet graveyards, and no one remembers exactly who they were or how they were related, if at all.

I Buried Three Babies In One Week

I didn't do much but rock sick babies when the diphtheria came in 1889. I rocked with one baby in my lap, one on my shoulder and listened for the breathing of the baby sleeping nearby. Adie died in my lap. She died just before dawn when the dark was thick deep and silent. I heard her last sigh. The baby, David, was sleeping on my shoulder. I kept rocking. Nancy whimpered in her cradle. I rocked her cradle with my hand. I was crying and my tears were rolling onto David. Adie was still cradled in my arm. She looked like she was asleep. I talked to her. I told her all the things we would have done. I prayed. I cried. I rocked us all so gently. I did not want to wake Ed. It was as if she were not really dead until I waked her daddy.

I rocked until Tad woke and took Adie from my arms. He held her for a long time himself. Then he laid her out in a blanket on our bed. That was only the beginning of the dying. We buried all three children within one week in October. It was a terrible time.

Aunt Kacky's Funeral

Aunt Kacky was a tall, thin, quiet woman who survived the Depression, three unnecessary shock treatments, and Grandma. Cousin Teeny swears Aunt Kacky was quiet because of the little purple pills Aunt Anne kept giving her. Every time I suggest this is an exaggeration. Teeny gets Aunt Mutt on the phone, who assures me that Aunt Anne did give Aunt Kacky a lot of pills, but the pills were orange and they seemed to keep Aunt Kacky content.

Aunt Kacky was the eldest child of Emma Lynn Rozzelle, and that had to be similar to being the firstborn of Attila the Hun's sister. She lost her purpose for living when her husband, Uncle Austin, died. Uncle Austin lost his job at the Ford plant during the Depression, causing them to lose their mortgaged home. This wouldn't have been so bad except it meant they had to move back home next to Grandma Emma, who hadn't had an easy life either. The Depression detoured many lives.

Austin made Aunt Kacky laugh all the years they were married. After he died, she ran a debit on laughter. During the1950s, they sat in two wooden rocking chairs by a wood-burning stove on bare linoleum and watched Jackie Gleason on a small black-and-white television, except on stormy nights when the angels moved heaven's furniture. Then they went to bed early and he held her tight until the storm rumbled off into the distance. Life was plowing with stubborn mules, hard work, peanuts and grits, but she was loved.

She never stopped grieving for her husband. Many people said it was because she didn't have anybody to boss around after Uncle Austin died. But I think it was because she didn't have anybody to love. I sat with them some nights, ate peanuts, and listened to Uncle Austin's soft fat belly chuckles along with the laugh track on television. They enjoyed the simple life.

Her grief seemed to make her vulnerable to family remedies that included three unnecessary shock treatments at Broughton Mental Hospital. But I lived far away then and I am not sure what took place. I do know the family and the doctors all meant well. It was a sad time. I had moved home by the time Aunt Kacky died. She died alone during a thunderstorm. I like to think Uncle Austin put his arms around her and took her home.

On the appointed day when her grieving had come to an end, after she had been taken away, pumped with chemicals and painted in unnatural colors, her kin gathered outside the church for her funeral.

When they began to sing, "Let the Circle Be Unbroken," we walked in pairs down the center aisle past the standing mourners to honor a woman who had survived upon this earth for seventy some years through some damned hard storms. But that is not exactly what happened.

The preacher meant well and I am sure he was paying Aunt Kacky a compliment when he compared her life to the act of dropping a white handkerchief from the heavens and it floating gently through the clouds of life. And now she was to be committed to dust, which would have a tremendous relief to Aunt Kacky, considering some of the places she had been committed. But those of us who were listening took umbrage with his handkerchief metaphor.

I heard my sister Anne ask, "What did he say?" Her husband replied, "I don't know." Cousin Rusty, Aunt Kacky's only child, began to sob even more loudly. Then I heard Anne ask again, only louder, "What did he say?" Obviously, she thought her hearing had gone bad.

From the far left of the row behind Anne, Cousin Yvonne answered in a train caller's whisper, "Something about a handkerchief?"

Then Yvonne returned to arguing with her daughter, Teeny. Only God knew exactly what they were arguing about or how it happened and only He remembers.

Us relatives kept hearing words they spit at each other between clenched teeth....

"Grounded fooor liiiife."

"Oh no, you don't."

"You will never drive my car again."

"Ummmph!! I'll show you."

"Idiot."

"Witch."

"I'll show you who is a witch."

Meanwhile the preacher was meandering between Psalms and the Sermon on the Mount, generally trying to draw everyone's attention from the immediate family mourners who were taking an ugly turn. It was too late; he had lost them at "handkerchief."

As we filed out that late fall day and began life without Aunt Kacky, my sister Anne immediately walked up to me and made me swear that I would never let anyone refer to the days of her life as a handkerchief dropped from heaven. She turned to leave, but came back and got in my face again and said, "Did you hear me? No handkerchiefs."

Yvonne stomped up to me to talk about stupid, unappreciative, spoiled children. Daddy and Uncle Harrison tried to make polite conversation with the preacher as car doors slammed and engines grumbled to life. Yvonne and I went to the twenty-four-hour convenience store, bought a gallon of cheap wine and when we were tipsy, we recalled our wonderful times with Aunt Kacky and Uncle Austin in a most irreverent way and blew our noses on white handkerchiefs.

Judy Rozzelle

Southern Grieving Is Unpredictable

Funerals are not always sad events in the South. Southern funerals can be downright memorable. The collision of our lust for living and the stark reality of death occasionally creates a spontaneous performance of theatre in the round.

My ex-sister-in law loved to tell of her grandfather's funeral. He had stopped attending the local Baptist church many years before his death, but when he died his wife decreed that his funeral was to be at the very church he had forsaken.

The preacher began the grandfather's eulogy by stating that he had fallen from grace and was doomed to hell. As the preacher paused for his next condemnation, the deceased's son stood up and motioned the family to assist him.

Together they pushed the casket out of the church with the son hollering: "My father would rise up and kill me if I let him lay there and listen to that crap." As the family paraded up the aisle pushing the casket, the young granddaughter waved at the gathered mourners, who sat in stunned silence. The preacher hollered to her father, "You are taking your family to hell also, son. Bring your father back up here and repent. Now."

This was the same family that painted their house pink and white to celebrate its eldest daughter's wedding and became Catholics.

Abby Rozzelle

Words Of Comfort

William Rozzelle was one of the nicest men I ever knew. He was always polite and he always made you feel good. When Dad died, William came by the house to pay his respects and, as he left, he shook my hand and looked in my eyes and said, "I will miss your father. He was my friend."

In those few words, he told me how deep their friendship was and it gave me comfort. I will never forget that.

Jarrell Cameron

Mary Alice Abernethy's Final Request

I went up to see Mary Alice Abernethy right before she died at 92. Her mind was sharp as a tack and she could still tell jokes. Just before I left, she told me she didn't want any men pallbearers at her funeral.

"If they couldn't take me out when I was alive, I don't want them carrying me to my final rest," she told me.

Lee Wallace

Seeking Comfort

One January evening, when the wind was stiff and the night was as dark as the inside of a pocket, Teeny called, sobbing into the phone around eleven p.m. We were all beginning to face the reality of Yvonne's illness. Teeny was distraught.

"Mom is up at her house alone and sick. I've got a sick child and can't go up to her house to check on her, but I am worried about her being alone. Please go check on her. Don't tell her I was worried," she pleaded. She was still loudly sobbing as she hung up the phone.

I was dressed comfortably, casually, and felt no need to change clothes. I was only going to Yvonne's as I had done a million times. I shoved my arms into my black wool blazer and left.

But I decided to stop in at the twenty-four-hour convenience store, built where Mamie and Esther's house once stood, for a pack of cigarettes. I swung open the door and blinked into the store's stark white lights. I asked Bert, the quiet gray bearded man who worked the night shift, how he was doing.

Bert wore his usual, a gold corduroy vest, plaid shirt, and faded jeans. It was his uniform. He smoked a pipe and always smelled of cherry tobacco. He had an easy smile, a big trusting face and bad teeth. Untold stories hovered about him like smoke. He laid the cigarette pack on the counter. I handed him a five-dollar bill and he gave me change.

I turned to leave and noticed strangers, newcomers to the area, staring at me. You could always tell they were new to country living. Their casual clothes were from Eddie Bauer catalogues and the garments matched. You knew they avoided caffeine and sodium and had never tasted beef jerky. I am sure they belonged to an exercise gym somewhere.

But this time, they were studying my stunning attire. I have always understood the true meaning of comfortable attire. Wearing comfortable clothing is an art of personal expression and, on that cold January night, I was a work of art and personal expression. I stood before them wearing orange furry bedroom slippers, green tights, an extra large purple nightshirt adorned with a huge Mickey Mouse silhouette and a black monogrammed blazer. We stared at each other.

"Hey," I called in their direction as I bolted out the door.

I slipped back into the car, stuck the keys into the ignition, drove 300 yards, and turned into Cousin's driveway. She heard the familiar *clomp, clomp* across her wooden porch and I am sure she knew it was me, but she looked out the side of the window blind just to make sure.

In the same movement, she unlocked the door, turned and headed back to her blankets on the couch as I entered. Wrapping and tucking them around her body, she settled back into her cocoon.

I collapsed onto the rug in front of her and say, "Well, I just became local color. Want to hear about it?"

She looked at me. She had a special intense look and a habit of sniffing her nose for no particular reason. Then she shook her head and smiled.

We talked into the night. The shadow of death stepped aside while we visited. We spoke softly, as people once did late at night, that quiet time when dew slumbers across the grass and the late night talk shows enter the void. This was a pause just before the land and its occupant's stretch, take a deep breath, turn off the lights and go to bed. We spoke of many things as the wind blew outside, but never of dying.

Judy Rozzelle

Yvonne And Harry Died Young

My cousins, Yvonne Rozzelle Herbert and Harry Rozzelle, died at forty-nine and fifty-four, both from cancer. Yvonne lived with her parents until at the age of forty-five. She built her English Tudor-style home at the end of a footpath not 100 yards from their house in what once was her mother's flower garden.

Harry never left home for more than a weekend except to go fishing or to a stock car race. He kept company with a patient and kind lady named Hazel for twenty-three years. He loved her dearly and took good care of her, but he wasn't leaving his parents. It was simply how he chose to live his life.

Yvonne died far from home in Washington, D.C., where she had gone for a last-chance cancer treatment. Her body was flown home and she missed the connection in Atlanta, which she had done many times in her life, but this missed flight caused her to be late for her own wake.

There were hundreds of people lined up to say goodbye when they rolled her casket into the receiving room. Yvonne would have loved it. Her final entrance hushed conversation and took the mourners' breath away.

I promised her I would make sure her fingernails were painted before the casket was closed. She had reminded me of this promise several times in the previous month. I carried nail polish in my pocketbook and whipped it out each time she mentioned it. This made us laugh.

But when the time came, I could not do it. I stayed in the room while someone else painted her nails her favorite color whorehouse red.

Harry did not die alone. His momma, Hazel, his niece Teeny, Cotton, a nurse, the minister and I were with him. Teeny kept talking in his ear as he departed.

"Everything will be all right. You can go to sleep now. I love you. Oh Harry, you were so good to all of us. We will miss you, but we don't want you to suffer any more. We'll be okay, but we will always love you."

I had tears running down my cheeks. My heart was breaking. I was losing another dear cousin.

Then Teeny said, "Harry, if you see Mom, would you tell her I love her and that I miss her. I miss my mother every day."

It was the first time I had been with someone when they died, and I was struck by the ordinariness of death. We were rushed away the moment he died and told to go home. It is so strange to just leave, pay your parking fee, and drive through streets watching folks rush hither and yon just like nothing had happened. The reality of death does not set in until the funeral is over, the friends have all gone, the last pie plate is washed. Then the void that is left comes in and sits down.

Judy Rozzelle

Arsonist Destroys The Rozzelle Ferry Inn

Just before midnight, August 28, 1990, an arsonist torched The Rozzelle Ferry Inn and Restaurant, and relegated it to ashes. My family's centuries old home place, now a North Carolina Historic Landmark was burned into history.

The fire siren at Sloan Volunteer Fire Department wailed into the darkness and the firemen rushed to the river to save another foundation. Their effort was mighty, but the kerosene had been poured thick in each room.

In the morning mists, Rozzelles descended on the ruins and carried away everything imaginable. Cousin Abby called for heavy equipment and had every foundation rock, including carriage stepping-stones, moved to the fields behind Shuffletown Grocery. She arranged them in a circle and designated them Shuffletown Stonehenge.

My last memory of the house was standing among the charred oak and solid timber while Barbara pointed to where the kerosene was splashed on the last remaining walls. It was an odious stain and I could feel the motions of the arsonist as he slung destruction all about the place. I could see the match drop and hear the roar of hungry flames as they rushed to feed on the kerosene soaked walls. We were standing in the large dining room where thousand of meals had been served to travelers for more than 100 years.

Just after sunset, my brother, Will Rozzelle, had a heart attack from exertion. We rushed from the ruins to the hospital. He survived to become the family historian as befitting the man named after the original owner of the house.

Everyone took home an artifact. I became the owner of three 200-year old ancestor Doric columns that now stand on my patio. The fourth column was placed at the entrance to Shuffletown Stonehenge.

The land where the house once stood is now a vacant lot except for the stone house where ice was once stored. Cousin Kissey used to tell our parents' generation about watching men cut ice from the river and carry it to the stone house.

It looks ancient, stalwart and vulnerable. It is a place lost in time. There resides this odd moss covered dwelling, standing on a knoll by the riverbank with motorboats and skidoos whizzing past, this unnoticed sentinel of history lost, marks time in the present, and waits for its future to be chronicled.

Judy Rozzelle

Henrietta Somers' Funeral

Henrietta Somers, 87, died three days after Hurricane Hugo struck Charlotte. My brother and I were in the pasture trying to cut down a pecan tree that had been damaged by the storm. When we saw the VFD emergency truck going down the Dead End Road, I knew.

"Something has happened to Henrietta," I said to Will. We both left our chore and ran over to her home. She had been frying a slice of fatback and sausage for breakfast when she suffered a stroke. Jenny discovered her on the floor when she came over to borrow a hat for church.

The funeral was held on a warm September day, I picked up my beloved nanny, Tommie Somers, and took her to the funeral to say goodbye to her sister-in-law. The church was packed with mourners and golden flowers.

We stood as Jenny and G-G entered the church. They were resplendent in white outfits. Each wore gloves and huge white hats. Aged and feeble, each sister was supported by ushers as they slowly came down the aisle whimpering into their handkerchiefs.

I had noticed that there were three robed ministers on the podium. When the funeral preaching began, I immediately became concerned about getting home in time for Christmas. The three preachers were intent on out preaching each other and ushering Henrietta to the glory of her great reward with a thousand hallelujahs. But you know it is not a bad thing in this world to stop and take time to send people off to their great final resting place. I just wonder why we don't take more time with people while they are alive.

Judy Rozzelle

Visiting Jenny For The Last Time

They are taking Jenny away tomorrow to a nursing home where she will die. They will latch the back door to her home from the inside, close the front door and lock it. Tomorrow or some day soon, someone will stake a "for sale" sign in the front yard. I am going to say goodbye today. It could be the last time I see her.

Daisy is to meet me at Jenny's as quickly as we both can get there after work. It is a magical April day. The land is painted in chartreuse green and the trees are budding in pink, white and cherry. Jenny always told me that spring blossoms and a litter of kittens are God's promise that the hard winter has passed.

The wooden steps creaked and bent as I stepped on them, moaning like all old things. The tin roof of her house has aged and rusted from the years it has sheltered those inside from the elements.

I rang the doorbell and pulled to open the door before I remembered to go around back. The back steps are even shakier.

I banged on the plywood patched screen door with the palm of my hand and hollered, "Hello."

While I waited for a response, I turned to look out across the neglected backyard. It is a forgotten place; flowers once tended and nurtured struggle to grow among strong eager weeds. Old fashioned plants, chicks and hens, lavender bushes, wild growing irises and tiny wild roses crept up remnants of what once was a fence.

But the most amazing sight was the oak tree and the wisteria vine. The wisteria vine had begun as a small intrusion between the roots of the tree, but it had grown to the size of an elephant's trunk and was wrapped as tightly around the tree as Scarlett O'Hara's corset.

The large purple wisteria blooms hung like bunches of grapes from the oak's limbs. Yet the old tree was filled with new green leaves. The parasite and the provider were both healthy, content and thriving in what could have been a bad relationship.

Only Daisy, still in her white uniform, snapping open the old latch brought me back to this goodbye place.

"Jenny's cold," she said, "I got the heat turned up." I understood.

There is a kinship between old folks and their oil stove. The older they get, the higher they turn up the heat and the closer they sit by the stove. Their rooms are stifling; it often feels like you have stepped into a preheated oven. It takes a moment to catch your breath. These are forgotten rooms where old people sit and dream backwards.

Jenny smiled as I entered. I dropped on one knee in front of her wheelchair and smiled into her eyes. Her eyes were as warm and comforting as liquid chocolate.

"How you doing?" she asked. "How is your daddy?"

Dad died ten years ago, but I had long stopped reminding Jenny of this dreary fact.

"He is fine," I lied, as I moved to sit in the yellow armchair embroidered with faded peach colored blossoms. Daisy dropped into a straight-backed chair and Jenny rolled nearer the oil stove that was radiating out heat into a 90-degree room.

Jenny dropped her head almost onto her chest and re-enters her silent reverie. Jenny was bent forward and even in the wheel chair seemed to be in a fetal position. Her false teeth were too large for her mouth. Her dirty blue skirt and worn red shoes were from a discount mart. Her old wig was loose on her head.

I cupped Jenny's tiny hands between mine. They were shrunken by a lifetime of scrubbing and rinsing. Each finger was bent, swollen and soaked with arthritis. Her skin hung loosely on her hands and to the touch it felt like soft brown silk. I had taken her hands to comfort her, but instead they comforted me.

"How was your day, Daisy?" I asked.

"Fine, one of the kids has a bad cold and I spent most of the day taking care of him."

"Do you know who this is?" she asked Jenny.

Jenny raised her head and replied indignantly, "This is Judy."

She had forgotten most everything she ever knew. But she knew at that moment who I was. "Judy looks just like her mother."

We laughed.

There was quiet for a moment as Daisy and I let go of the workday and eased into the moment, settling into old ways and this sad day.

Jenny dropped back into yesterday and touched the brown enamel of the stove. The single bed was the old four-poster bed I slept in as a child and it was covered with a worn quilt made long before I was born. There was a framed photograph of her home on the nightstand. I had taken the photo one fall when it was framed by golden trees, and framed it in an orange wooden frame for her Christmas present.

On the nightstand sat an old white hobnailed lamp. The shade was so old that the original color was undistinguishable. A digital clock with large loud numbers sat between the photo and the lamp. It was totally out of sync in this museum of a room. Daisy and Ivy's phone numbers were written on white paper in large bold letters and taped to the wall by the nightstand. Like all of us, these are no relation to Jenny except the bonds formed through sharing life as neighbors and friends. But Ivy and Daisy had cared for Jenny daily for the past five years. I regret to say that I have not been so faithful.

A portable potty was pushed into the corner with a bath rug hung over it.

Jenny was back to using a chamber pot, but now she didn't have to slide it back under the bed.

Jenny raised her head and asked, "Judy, what are they doing to Shuffle? Have you seen those big bulldozers on your daddy's property?"

"Things are changing, Jenny," I answered.

"I don't understand why they are changing Shuffletown. It was a pretty good place to live."

"I know, Jenny. It was a wonderful place to live."

"It sure was," Daisy laughed. "Everybody got along. They made us kids go to different schools, but we didn't much know we was different until the school bus arrived."

"That's cause we were all farmers' kids and we didn't know any difference," I replied.

"We shared back and forth with each in the good times and the bad. Mrs. Nixon brought us buttermilk whenever her cow came fresh," continued Daisy. "Momma did the same."

"Does your daddy know they pushed trees and dirt into the old pond?" Jenny asked.

"Everything is different now, Jenny," I answered, "I sure wish it wasn't, but it is." She looked like a small brown sparrow and I wanted so to take her home and make her young again. I wanted to cry. But if I did, I feared long sobs would roll out of my throat.

"Does Mr. Tad still run the store? Where is your brother? They tore his house down." Jenny's questioning eyes searched my face for an answer.

"Abby runs the store for Uncle Tad, now. Will and Barbara moved up to the lake and they are going to build a big grocery store where the pond was." I cupped her small hands and patted them lightly.

"'Sho nuff," she answered. "They'll never get Anne to move away," she said with a smile. "Anne won't leave Shuffle."

"Things haven't been right around here since they burned down Mamie and Esther's house and built the twenty-hour gas station," I said, as I winked at Jenny.

"Jenny, do you remember the time you kept me from beating up Tony Huffstetler when he took Brad's bike?" I asked.

"I sure do," She answered. A spark of memory made her smile. "Judy, you was always a mess. But I almost paddled you that day right in front of your children.

"I had just gotten home from work and Brad came running into the house hollering that Tony Huffstetler had taken his bike away from him. Again.

"I had just slipped off my dress and I was standing in the kitchen in my slip talking to Jenny. Tony Huffstetler was a bully and three years older than Brad. This time it flew all over me and I headed out the door hollering for Tony to get over here. I was halfway to his house when Jenny caught up with me. Jenny was screaming for me to put my clothes on and Brad was screaming that he would run away from home if I beat up Tony."

Jenny was laughing and shaking her head. "You were a mess."

"You made me stand behind a big old tree in Will's yard and put on my dress." I leaned on Jenny's shoulder and wept.

"Jenny, I love you so much. Thank you for being part of my life."

We sat in silence, the three of us in a worn-out house in a worn-out room mourning a worn-out time.

Judy Rozzelle

Leaving Jenny's

Daisy walked out with me when I had spoken the last goodbye to Jenny. We walked around the overgrown yard musing about this and that. We strolled over to the backyard behind Henrietta's house. Her house has stood empty since 1990. No one has spent the night there since the Sunday morning Henrietta dropped dead at 89 while she was frying fatback and sausage for breakfast. After the funeral, Jenny and G-G wouldn't hear of cleaning out the house or renting it. They just locked the door and checked the house everyday as if Henrietta was expected home at anytime.

Daisy opened the door to an old shed behind the house. I noticed an old faded hatbox full of books, discarded tin pots and iron frying pans. I stepped inside, picked up the hatbox, and stuffed it with some books.

Suddenly, the air changed. It felt like we were being watched. Both of us became spooked.

Daisy said, "I believe there are ghosts in here. Come on out?"

"Daisy, if anything moves or speaks to us, I'll try not to run over you getting out of here. But you had better move out of the way fast or I might," I said.

A few minutes later, as the sun began to set, we were picking flowers from a wild place that was once a garden. As dusk settled across the land, we were both clutching the stems of purple irises and yellow daffodils. I held tightly to the rope handle of the old hatbox filled with books.

For some reason I set the box down and walked back to look at a wild spreading rosebush with Daisy. When I turned to leave, we couldn't find the old hatbox. We looked around and behind bushes. Then we saw it set far away in a place we had not been.

"You better grab that hatbox and go," Daisy said, "before we see a ghost."

As I was leaving, I looked at the old black windowpanes of Henrietta's house, but the ghost I saw in my mind's eye was Henrietta waving goodbye. If I had lingered a moment longer, I am sure I would have heard Momma call me to supper.

Judy Rozzelle

Jenny's Eulogy

I am here today with my family and friends to honor the life of Jenny Grant Owen. Jenny grew up like my father and mother in a time when life was lived in rhythm with the changing seasons in a place called Shuffletown. Like many of us, Jenny could recall a time when tomatoes tasted like summer and things were built just so. It was an era when fields were for planting not parking lots.

She was born when the previous century was new. Her father, Elijah Grant, owned and farmed 35 acres of land in Shuffletown. I recently asked, a Shuffletown old timer, if he remembered her parents, Elijah and Hattie Grant. He said he certainly did. He recalled that Elijah Grant was widely respected for his hard work, his wit and his wisdom.

When November and hog killing season came around Elijah Grant was in high demand. It seems that no one else for miles around could best Elijah when it came to butchering a hog and knowing how to best preserve the meat. Elijah and his wife had three daughters, Jenny, GG and Henrietta. At that time, babies were carried into the fields in baskets, when they were old enough to crawl out of the basket, they were taught how to gather and pick the harvest.

Hank Wallen recalled that Elijah's daughters could drive a mule and plow as good as a man, even though they were small women. Several hot summers ago, Jenny and GG told me of the spring drought in 1936. I remember GG telling me that six weeks after she had placed the seeds in the ground, you could walk among the rows, brush aside the dirt and the seed was still dry as a bone. It did not rain until mid-June that year. Farmers were in the fields that year and did not have time to celebrate the fourth of July.

Jenny, at the age of fourteen, learned to drive her father's Model A Ford. It was not an uncommon sight to see the car rattling down dirt roads with Jenny driving. She peered through the steering wheel, not above it, to see the road. Jenny once told me the old car never had headlights, but that did not matter as she never had the nerve to drive at night.

Jenny and her sisters were always close. When Henrietta's husband died, she had her house moved a mile down the road and set it down beside Jenny and GG's house. When the nights were hot and humid and the air was still, they would talk to each other from their bedroom windows until they fell asleep.

Jenny and her sisters cared for the ailing and the young. Jenny taught the young ones in Shuffletown to mind the good book and keep the Ten Commandments...as their parents had taught them.

When GG was dying, Jenny never left her side. Her days were lonely after Henrietta and GG died, but she was still spunky. Her faith and her church sustained her.

Jenny and the Grant family were our neighbors and our friends. As the years passed they took their place as our respected elders. Their lives intertwined with ours as it always happens in small places.

In this new millennium, Jenny has left quietly as she once entered in a new century. It is not uncommon in this time of change and progress to bid goodbye to many dear and gentle people and small communities. It is a time of change, but we can honor their passing and promise to remember, always.

For the kids who came calling on Halloween for Jenny's homemade popcorn treats, for William and Josephine Rozzelle and all her other Shuffletown friends who departed before her and all the lives she graced...may I say thank you, Jenny, you were our friend. I know God sent a band of angels to bring you home.

Judy Rozzelle

I Am Witness

In the spring of 1998, while driving home from work, I noticed that the Plummer family, as they have done for many decades, had staked a scarecrow in their garden. But this summer, the torn farmer's clothes and ragged straw hat on a post were not enough to scare off a subdivision going up only a few hundred yards from the corn and tomato plants.

Then my sister and brother began to carefully talk to me about selling the homeplace. I could not afford to fix up the house and burglars were beginning to break into the house on a regular basis...always about a month after I replaced the computer and the television.

In June 2000, we sold. I moved from my home to Coulwood. This dear house built by my parents in 1930 stood empty for the first time in 70 years. Doors, windows, mantles were hauled away to become heirlooms. We stripped the house, leaving only the shell of what had once been home.

Cold winds blew through the kitchen where I, in a time before, impatiently waited for biscuits and supper. Frost fills the chimney and the front entrance, empty of its secure oak door, stares out onto the highway like an unblinking eye. I turned away from its gaze each time I passed by on the highway.

On December 23, 2000, bulldozers pushed my home into yesterday. Like locusts, yellow bulldozers descended on this ground, pushing, leveled the knoll where my home once stood to make way for the shopping center to be called Rozzelles Crossing. The pond behind the house was drained. The red barn was knocked down; the other houses on the property were destroyed and hauled away.

Now, discarded Styrofoam, beer cans and bright cellophane wrapper litter the ditches. Homes that once enjoyed solitude at the end of long driveways or the top of a hill are prey to thieves and robbers.

Gardens lush with night-blooming cereus have given way to 24-hour convenience stores and grab-and-go restaurants.

Folks who once enjoyed mowing an acre yard are now to frail to pull the lawnmower out of the garage. Their children live too far away to help with the upkeep of the homestead. Many have sold their parents' land. More are negotiating to sell, or waiting on higher prices.

This crossroads community, once thriving with crops and cousins, is little more than a collection now of abandoned clapboard houses. The infection of progress has taken hold; I am helpless to stop its spread.

Memories of places, and people must be told and told again until they become family legends and myths. Generations of Rozzelles, Gillises, Griffins and Camerons yet unborn must know from hearing the stories that there was a place called Shuffletown and of those who called it home.

I am witness to the passing of an era. I am witness to the disappearance of Shuffletown, USA. I am witness to the end of the American rural tradition of communities and towns.

Judy Rozzelle

I Never Listen To Willie Nelson Alone

Even now, Yvonne is always with me when Willie sings. After Elvis Presley died, Willie Nelson was her favorite crooner. She would have run away with him…anywhere, anytime, if he had asked. She thought this crooner with a face like a wrinkled map, was sexy. Maybe it was his pigtails, but I think it was his song lyrics. Nobody sings of "What once was…or what could have been" quite like Willie.

Yvonne and I had a favorite time to listen to him. Late at night, usually we were in the car on our way home from either a movie or dinner with friends. As the road to Shuffletown stretched into the night's darkness, we would pop in a tape, and do something rare. We would melt into silence.

Sometimes, we listened to Presley, Joplin, Temptations, but most often, this time was reserved for Willie. His song *Stardust* was good, but our favorite was *Faded Love*. The silence became soft when Willie crooned about faded memories and lost love.

On one occasion, I was driving the dark-wine colored Buick I drove when I worked at Bob Dill's advertising agency. It was later than usual. The movie had run long or we had dallied longer than usual at Gary and Roger's house.

Back then, there were great long stretches of countryside on the road out to Shuffletown with only occasional porch lights peering into the night. The crossroads were quieter then, and usually deserted by midnight. On this night, as I approached the turn onto Mt. Holly-Huntersville Road, instead of turning right to take her home I continued on Rozzelles Ferry Road to the river.

It was an unspoken agreement. We needed to listen to *Faded Love* one more time in silence. We crossed the bridge named for our ancestors over the age-old waters, but we were each far away in our thoughts.

We had reached the age of reflection and this song helped our souls to cry. For a few more minutes we remained in that place a car takes you that place of "betwixt and between." Here life hangs suspended between beginning and continuing. The song ended as we passed the end of the bridge. I turned the car around at the mouth of a worn, littered road by the river. Where teenagers parked to neck, I turned the car around, drove back across the bridge, and took her home.

I never listen to Willie Nelson alone. Just as he sucks in air and begins to sing, Yvonne slips into the room and has a seat. She is smiling. It is dark and we are driving down the highway.

Judy Rozzelle

Yvonne's Granddaughter

In honor of her grandmother, Erin Elizabeth Henderson now looks and acts like Yvonne Rozzelle Herbert. There is little that scares Erin Elizabeth. At ten years old, she speaks her mind; she would rather ride her horse than comb her hair. Erin Elizabeth was only two months old when Yvonne succumbed to cancer. It is as if Yvonne whispered to Erin Elizabeth what was important in life and what was not important the last time she held her.

Also, in honor of her grandmother and other Rozzelle relatives she has the skinniest ankles in the county. Slick Cameron and Jim Bob have asked her, "Are those your legs? Or are you riding a chicken?"

Yvonne and I heard that question a lot in years long gone by.

Judy Rozzelle

The Family Pond

The developers broke the dam and drained the pond in September. Almost an acre of water slipped away, leaving mud and drowning fish. The pond and its wildness was a special place governed only by nature. Dad built the pond in the 40s so the cows would always have water and we would have a place to fish. Someone once told me the pond was fed by five springs. If this is the case, cement will not set in this place.

When the pond was fresh and new, the water was as clear as drifting glass. Dad stocked the pond with bass and bream. Mother taught me to sit quietly by the water's edge and watch. I swear, I saw fish spawn in those translucent waters. I saw female fish squirm about in the mud to lay their eggs, and then the male swam over the eggs and fertilized this new life. It was a dance, a ritual, known by rote.

For many springtimes I squatted by the pond's edge to watch for new beginnings. Have you ever watched a tadpole become a frog? The black little tadpoles begin life as a swirling school of black specks. When they are about two inches long they are beautiful little darting black fish with fins and fancy tails. First they lose their tails and their fins change to lungs. Soon little feet appear and they jump to the pond's edge. Before you know it, bullfrogs surround the water, calling in deep booming voices to welcome summer.

Inch-long insects we called snake doctors, but most folks call them dragonflies, darted about the shore. They hovered like helicopters by cattails and other water grasses and then flew to another curiosity. It was on these banks, by the water's edge, that I began to believe in magic.

The dam, where the water was the deepest, was my favorite part of the pond. You could tell how dry the weather had been by how much of the dam was showing above the pond's drainpipe. Trees grew all along the perimeter of the pond except on the dam. Just grass grew on the dam. In the more than fifty years the pond existed, only one straggling tree grew on the dam. This tree grew in the middle of the dam right on the water's edge. It was half-anchored on land and half rooted in the water, part water lily and part pine. This tree never grew to be large or even straight. It seemed embarrassed it had even tried to grow in this odd place. It grew out across the water staring at its reflection.

By mid-summer a green carpet of algae grew across the water. Dad threw fertilizer on it in an attempt to kill it. He skimmed it off and threw it into the woods behind the pond. But the green algae persisted and as the seasons changed it dropped to the bottom of the pond to feed the fish in the wintertime.

In winter, a thin layer of ice sealed the pond waters. We stopped swimming in the pond, but it was always a good place for the whole community to fish. The pond was a place to be thoughtful.

Green herons were known to visit these waters, and twice I saw a migrating water turkey. This odd bird had a snaky s-shaped neck. It dove deep into the water seeking fish and sat on high tree limbs to shake its wings dry. In the last decades, several pairs of geese hatched goslings. As nesting parents, the geese hissed and squawked away any daring intruder. When the goslings stepped out of the nest, the geese patiently walked the goslings along the shore and taught them to search for insects and seeds. By late fall they flew into the autumn sky.

We built forts and played pretend among the pines. Under adult supervision, we built bonfires and stoked them with branches. When the fire grew hot and sure, we stuck hot dogs on straightened wire coat hangers and roasted them in the fire. We sat in the light of the fire and told ghost stories, as the dark behind us grew dense and deep. No one walked home alone.

My dogs, Skipper and Whiskey, rested in the pet cemetery by the pond, along with Will's dog, Snookie, and my sister's infinite number of deceased cats.

Mother planted daffodils on the banks of the pond and they multiplied like rabbits each spring. After her passing their yellow trumpets were a reminder of her. Sister dug up the golden bulbs and carried them away when we sold the property.

The pond was a canvas, a backdrop for our lives. I will not walk across the hill to where it once settled its watery presence. I do not care to. Sometimes, when I am driving by the road, I steal a glimpse in the direction of where this sacred waters once flowed and the trees that stood firm along its banks lean in sorrow by this punctured place like mourners at a graveside.

Judy Rozzelle

Annie Beth Nixon Ends An Era

In every family, there are unexplainable chance occurrences, the kind of coincidences that escape notice in cities, but which people in small towns remember, and recount. These remnants of astounding events are passed from cousin to cousin, sister to sister, neighbor to neighbor. It is an oral tradition stoked and stirred for a time by one event and then forgotten until another coincidence prods the old folks to start remembering again.

Annie Beth Nixon's death on July 4, 2000 was just such a coincidence.

Annie Beth Nixon, a lifelong resident of Shuffletown, died at home. Her death was sudden and sad, but, falling as it did on the nation's birthday, it was honored with a homespun display of fireworks.

Few of us knew Annie was dying. Her health had been failing for more than a month, and her daughters had been in town to see her, but it wasn't like Annie to say anything. She had her opinions, she knew how things ought to be, and, though it drove her daughters almost batty, she held tightly to the sovereignty of her life to the very end.

I saw her in the grocery store on a regular basis. She was always dressed in exercise outfits. These matching ensembles were made of unnatural material dyed in metallic blue and green. They certainly accentuated her short red hair. The fabric sighed each time she moved. Her tennis shoes were always perfectly unscuffed.

When her presence was missed at Harris Teeter, we exchanged our own opinions.

"It is a bad ear infection that is throwing her off balance."

"I heard she fell."

"Bad stomach ailment."

"I heard she was in the hospital."

Finally, it was told, "Annie Beth has cancer."

In fact, she had only weeks to live. But Annie Beth Nixon had decreed that she would not breathe her last in a hospital. There would be no life support or extraordinary efforts made to keep her alive. She would continue to get her hair fixed every week. She would get up every day, put on her makeup, and have breakfast. And she would continue to smoke.

She did agree to wait until the oxygen tanks were removed from the room before she struck a match.

I had been witness to two key events in Annie Beth's life, though I did not know her that well. I knew her mother had died soon after

153

she had been born. I knew her father, Mac Gillis, because he owned and operated the general store. It was in the corner of the crossroads, a one-story clapboard building with sawdust on the floor, penny candy in the glass counters, and sacks of flour and feed in the back. In the center of the store was a potbellied stove. He kept a wooden straight chair under a tree outside the building. In the afternoon, as shade spread out against the heat, he would lean his chair against the building, his chin against his chest, and nap.

The Gillis home was right next to the grocery, directly across the street from our house. From my bedroom on the second floor, I could study the Gillis's front porch. I spent many nights staring out across the dark road, into the Gillis's lives. That's how I came to witness Annie Beth Gillis kiss Jack Nixon goodnight after a date. I could see the silhouette of their heads, until Mac Gillis opened the front door.

The other key event was the burning of Mac Gillis's store. My mother woke me in the middle of the night to come see. When I ran into the night air, the blaze was hungry and billowing. I watched the flames leap through the roof, burning timber, melting chocolate, and wasting feed.

Our volunteer fire department had just been formed, but it was too late for them to act. The men stood watch to contain the fire and spare Mac Gillis's home. Mothers hugged children in silence.

And here is the coincidence: Mac Gillis's store burned to the ground before midnight on July 4, 1951.

Aunt Anne recalled the date of the fire. She reminded me of this when she called, on the Fourth, to tell me that Annie Beth was not expected to live out the day.

But it was Aunt Mutt who recalled that Annie Beth Nixon's mother died on July 4th, just weeks after Annie Beth's birth.

Annie Beth died that afternoon. She had not counted on departing so early because she had promised my ten-year-old cousin, Erin Elizabeth, that they would watch fireworks together through her bedroom window. Erin Elizabeth had gone with her father, Cotton, to South Carolina to purchase the fireworks. Annie Beth died before they returned.

Still, her daughters requested that the bags of fireworks not be wasted, that in honor of their mother, we have a display. So just after dark, several of us walked across the long front yard and settled on her front porch in white rocking chairs. We didn't talk much as the red and blue sparks flared in the blackness and whistled toward the stars.

Judy Rozzelle

The Final Invasion

The South has been invaded again. This time, we sold them the land and taught them how to eat grits and catfish. Now there are so many of them here they have moved out to Shuffletown and invaded our gene pool.

William Alexander Rozzelle V

All the Farms Are Gone

The time for plowing has passed and even the noise of the drag strip is long past. Now, I am just another old, bald, short Wallen with time on my hands.

Hank Wallen

No Place To Grow A Christmas Tree

The time has passed when the family Christmas tree was gathered from the woods or the pasture. There are no fallow cotton fields or flat bottomland where a cedar tree can grow into a proper tree. Everyone buys a Christmas tree from a lot these days. There have been so many changes and losses.

Jarrell Cameron

Time To Leave Shuffletown

There seem to be only two seasons these days. Summer is so hot it feels like you're standing too close to the stove and winter is either warmer and drier than usual or it is one ice storm after another. It makes you feel like you are living in an ice age. Spring and Fall have dwindled down to a couple of weeks of breathing space between the extremes of winter and summer.

I believe the trouble started with ten-digit local phone numbers, nine-digit zip codes and urban sprawl. Wild-eyed developers push down the old, put up the barely built new and pave over what's left. That's what happened to Shuffletown. The place is just like everywhere else now. I think it is time to move.

Bob Griffin

Stories Are The Torch

Stories are the torch, the eternal flame we pass from one generation to the next. They must be captured and told before the voices fall silent, before the details fade and the names are forgotten. For only in keeping the names alive do we keep the spirits with us. Without a record, without giving constant voice to the past, we condemn those who lived here to an eternity of silence in a forgotten graveyard.

Judy Rozzelle

The two little girls exist only in our minds and hearts now.
There is only a hole in the air and the wind of their passage.
So, it is with a place once called Shuffletown.

About Shuffletown, USA
Robert Tolan, Director, Generations Theatre Group

As Charlotte city limits move inexorably outward, a small crossroads village in northwest Mecklenburg County lies in the path of progress. This farming community, which grew up on the banks of the Catawba River in the early part of the 19th Century, is being bulldozed into oblivion. Shuffletown, a kind of American "Everytown," boasted more than its fair share of eccentrics as well as good, hard-working farmers and trades people. But the lifestyle that included free-range chickens on the roads, a Festival featuring a stationary parade, a fire department whose motto was "We never lose a foundation," an appliance repair shop filled with unclaimed items their owners couldn't stand to throw away, and a preacher who waited twenty-two years to marry a girl he baptized and fell in love with as a baby is only part of the story. A whole culture, a way of life, is being sacrificed to progress, and writer Judy Rozzelle (a fifth generation descendant of the Rozzelles Ferry Rozzelles) was determined that if Shuffletown itself was being lost, it would be saved in memory, for the sake of its children and their children's children.

About the Author

Judy Rozzelle has been a freelance writer since 1971. She sold the first article she ever wrote to Reader's Digest and has since published in several national magazines. She was a winner in the 1986 *Guideposts Writer's Contest*. As an outdoor writer, she was a member of the *Southeastern Outdoor Writer's Association*.

She was senior editor for *Charlotte Magazine*. The editor at that time was Jim Townsend, the father of great city magazines. At Charlotte Magazine, she met Jan Karon and Pat Conroy.

She was a partner in a locally infamous copywriting and promotions firm, Haley, Garland and Lahr. During this time, she and her partners traversed many yellow brick roads and developed some of the cleverest advertising lines ever conceived. A few times, they remembered to write them down.

In the previous decade, she served penance and worked for a financial institution answering letters from irate customers. This drove her to once again seek sanity in the world of writing. It may have been too late.

Ms. Rozzelle wrote this book in an effort to redeem herself in Shuffletown. She also felt bad because she never completed the history of the church in time for its centennial celebration in 1991.